D1254039

SocioDynamic Counselling:
A Practical Approach
To Meaning Making

R. Vance Peavy

Taos Institute

SOCIODYNAMIC COUNSELLING:
A PRACTICAL APPROACH TO MEANING MAKING

FIRST EDITION Copyright © 2004 by Judith Peavy
REPRINT Copyright © 2010 by Taos Institute Publications

This is to acknowledge the invaluable assistance of Melinda
Maunsell in the copy editing of this book.
The drawing on the front cover is entitled Life Mapping: Self
as Counsellor, and is the work of Karen Zemarek, M.Ed. candidate
in Counselling, University of Victoria, 1997. The drawing
was her response to an assignment in the course "SocioDynamic
Counselling" taught by Dr. R. Vance Peavy.

Library of Congress Catalog Card Number: 2003113309

Taos Institute Publications
A Division of the Taos Institute
Chagrin Falls, Ohio
USA

ISBN 0-9712312-4-9
ISBN-13: 978-0-9712312-4-5   Printed in the USA and in the UK

Taos Institute Publications

TA☉S
INSTITUTE
Publications

The Taos Institute is a nonprofit organization dedicated to the development of social constructionist theory and practice for purposes of world benefit. Constructionist theory and practice locate the source of meaning, value, and action in communicative relations among people. Our major investment is in fostering relational processes that can enhance the welfare of people and the world in which they live. Taos Institute Publications offers contributions to cutting-edge theory and practice in social construction. Our books are designed for scholars, practitioners, students, and the openly curious public. The **Focus Book Series** provides brief introductions and overviews that illuminate theories, concepts, and useful practices. The **Tempo Book Series** is especially dedicated to the general public and to practitioners. The **Books for Professionals Series** provides in-depth works, that focus on recent developments in theory and practice. Our books are particularly relevant to social scientists and to practitioners concerned with individual, family, organizational, community, and societal change.

Kenneth J. Gergen
President, Board of Directors
The Taos Institute

For information about the Taos Institute and social constructionism
visit: www.taosinstitute.net

Taos Institute Publications

Taos Tempo Series: Collaborative Practices for Changing Times

Ordinary Life Therapy: Experiences from a Collaborative Systemic Practice, (2009) by Carina Håkansson

Mapping Dialogue: Essential Tools for Social Change, (2008) by Marianne "Mille" Bojer, Heiko Roehl, Mariane Knuth-Hollesen, and Colleen Magner

Positive Family Dynamics: Appreciative Inquiry Questions to Bring Out the Best in Families, (2008) by Dawn Cooperrider Dole, Jen Hetzel Silbert, Ada Jo Mann, and Diana Whitney

Focus Book Series

The Appreciative Organization, Revised Edition (2008) by Harlene Anderson, David Cooperrider, Ken Gergen, Mary Gergen, Sheila McNamee, Jane Watkins, and Diana Whitney

Appreciative Inquiry: A Positive Approach to Building Cooperative Capacity, (2005) by Frank Barrett and Ronald Fry

Dynamic Relationships: Unleashing the Power of Appreciative Inquiry in Daily Living, (2005) by Jacqueline Stavros and Cheri B. Torres

Appreciative Sharing of Knowledge: Leveraging Knowledge Management for Strategic Change, (2004) by Tojo Thatchekery

Social Construction: Entering the Dialogue, (2004) by Kenneth J. Gergen, and Mary Gergen

Appreciative Leaders: In the Eye of the Beholder, (2001) edited by Marge Schiller, Bea Mah Holland, and Deanna Riley

Experience AI: A Practitioner's Guide to Integrating Appreciative Inquiry and Experiential Learning, (2001) by Miriam Ricketts and Jim Willis

Books for Professionals Series

Positive Approaches to Peacebuilding: A Resource for Innovators, (2010) edited by Cynthia Sampson, Mohammed Abu-Nimer, Claudia Liebler, and Diana Whitney

Social Construction on the Edge: 'Withness'-Thinking & Embodiment, (2010) by John Shotter

Joined Imagination: Writing and Language in Therapy, (2009) by Peggy Penn

Celebrating the Other: A Dialogic Account of Human Nature, (reprint 2008) by Edward Sampson

Conversational Realities Revisited: Life, Language, Body and World, (2008) by John Shotter

Horizons in Buddhist Psychology: Practice, Research and Theory, (2006) edited by Maurits Kwee, Kenneth J. Gergen, and Fusako Koshikawa

Therapeutic Realities: Collaboration, Oppression and Relational Flow, (2005) by Kenneth J. Gergen

SocioDynamic Counselling: A Practical Guide to Meaning Making, (2004) by R. Vance Peavy

Experiential Exercises in Social Construction – A Fieldbook for Creating Change, (2004) by Robert Cottor, Alan Asher, Judith Levin, and Cindy Weiser

Dialogues About a New Psychology, (2004) by Jan Smedslund

For on-line ordering of books from Taos Institute Publications visit
www.taosinstitutepublications.net

For further information, call: 1-888-999-TAOS, 1-440-338-6733
Email: info@taosoinstitute.net

Table of Contents

List of Figures

An Introduction
to Vance Peavy's Work

As a former student and colleague of Vance Peavy, I am honoured to be able to add my voice to his and to reflect on the impact of his ideas presented so elegantly in this book. Although Vance has focussed most of his scholarly work on the professional helping relationship, his work has much more relevance than the boundaries of traditional counselling practice. In addition to reflecting on his ideas, I also want to contextualize his work so that readers who may not be familiar with the discipline of counselling psychology will be able to see the value of his SocioDynamic perspective in their own work.

Since Vance's sudden death in July of 2002, much has occurred in the international arena and at home. Although September 11 still serves as a constant reminder of our collective vulnerability, this event merely foreshadowed other catastrophic events. The Bali bombings, the attack on Iraq, the current concern over alleged weapons programs in Iran and North Korea, are ongoing reminders that the world and our relations with it are far from harmonious. Reactions to these events are varied, prompting some people to become open to changing the ways in which we participate in international affairs and prompting others to return to a fundamentalist approach of clinging to what feels familiar despite its uncertainty. Whichever response is taken, certainly disengagement with these unsettling issues is not an option. More than any other time in history, our prolific connectivity due to technology makes it impossible to hide from the social, economic, and psychological impact of world events. And more than at any other time in history, we need to understand the complexities of co-constructing our lives together. These precarious and troubling times call into question how we can foster ways of relating that generate new possibilities, not corrective measures that position one reality against another.

Vance tackles these kinds of challenges, which makes his book particularly relevant for practitioners and others who want to understand how we engage in generative conversations both in clinical practice and in everyday life. He invites people to consider re-visioning counselling practice as a form of relating that fosters constructive dialogues, not oppressive monologues. In this spirit of openings to new possibilities, I want to highlight his work by organizing my reflections on three questions. First, how does SocioDynamic counselling fit with other counselling orientations? Second, in what ways does this particular way of relating to others address the complexities of postmodern life? And finally, who will benefit from reading and implementing these ideas?

How does SocioDynamic counselling fit with other counselling orientations?

Vance created the term *SocioDynamic* because of his belief in the social influence on the dynamic processes when constructing a self. By using this term, Vance was able to emphasize the relational aspect of human experience so that we can understand people, not by looking for an interior self found lurking in the psyche, but by understanding the social relationships we engage in and the cultural artifacts we use to construct a life. Because of this focus on the social context, a SocioDynamic perspective can be positioned alongside other relational approaches, such as Michael Mahoney's work in social constructivism, Ken and Mary Gergen's work[1] in social constructionist thinking, and certain modes of narrative thinking, such as those described by Jerome Bruner. The overall purpose of this book is to weave these theoretical orientations into a philosophical perspective on how to work with people's concerns in daily life. It is, therefore, a practical book that moves the reader gently through theoretical foun-

---

1. Ken and Mary Gergen's work on the self and dialogical communication had a major impact on Vance's thinking about professional helping. Many of their foundational concepts and ideas about relationship have important similarities

dations to pragmatic ways of working *with*, not *on*, people's life difficulties. In addition to being led through rich theoretical bodies of knowledge, you also will be introduced to philosophical ideas found in existential and humanistic psychology. Through his extensive reading in these traditions, Vance developed a strong belief in the indeterminacy of human life mixed with his equally strong belief in the capacity for resiliency of the human spirit.

You will notice that Vance has relied on several theories that are currently understood as postmodern. A belief in the self as multiple, co-created, narrative, and highly relational locates his work within this paradigm. There is a complementary relationship, therefore, between Vance's approach and those theories that recognize the challenges of postmodern life yet refuse to be immobilized or constrained by them. People, according to Vance, are social actors and moral agents who use language to construct complex, organized systems of meanings. Ideas, perspectives, and meanings profoundly influence how we act and negotiate our relations in and with the world.

There are also several connections between Vance's work and the perspectives adopted by those affiliated with the Taos Institute. Vance strongly believed in the transformative energy that occurs when people enter into dialogues that generate new meanings together, instead of monologues that tend to be individualistic. Dialogues, including words, symbols, images, and metaphors, are meaningless outside the context in which they arise. A similar perspective on the value of coordinated conversations can be found in the goals of the Taos Institute, where various forms of communication that foster connection, not disconnection, are valued and promoted. Truth is not born in, nor found inside the head of, an individual person; it is born between people who are collectively searching for multiple truths, in the process of their dialogic interaction. Vance also believed in the same kind of goals as appreciative inquiry,[2] where it is assumed that if we can work from a

2. See Cooperrider and Whitney, (1999). *A Positive Revolution in Change: Appreciative Inquiry*. Taos Institute Publication.

strengths-based perspective and consider what gives "life" to people, organizations, and societies, much untapped and rich accounts of people's lives can be used.

In what ways does this particular form of counselling address the challenges of contemporary life, such as the misunderstandings that occur due to ethnicity, gender, and socio-economic status?
During the past few decades, Western psychological knowledge has been criticized for its lack of attention to diversity. Certain types of multicultural and feminist psychology have been developed in response to these critiques. When Vance began to develop SocioDynamic counselling, he was fully aware of the need to develop an approach that was sensitive to difference, and he continuously cautioned helping professionals to avoid taking a difference-blind approach. Consequently, his approach (a) repositions the counsellor as coach or mentor, not as expert, (b) emphasizes the dialogical nature of the counselling process, and (c) highlights the cultural intelligence needed to work across differences. In my own work, I use the term *cultural attunement* to emphasize the need to listen carefully to the meanings that people make in relation to their ethnic and gendered identities. Vance and I agree wholeheartedly that there is no such thing as a cultural toolkit that can be used to understand how ethnic, gender, and socio-economic status have shaped a person's life story. Dialogical listening avoids the pitfalls that occur when people believe that they can essentialize certain minority groups. Vance recommends asking: Does the counselling process take advantage of the wisdom that is part of the cultural heritage of the help-seeker? Are the counsellor and help-seeker able to generate good ideas about what to do and how to proceed by drawing from the stock of knowledge they have as members of particular cultures?

Vance was convinced that if counsellors would follow the principles and practices outlined in this book, many of the oppressive practices that have permeated traditional counselling approaches could be avoided. This is not to say that specific, sometimes historical knowledge about certain groups of people is superfluous.

When I once confessed to Vance that I did not know very much about our First Nations people in our province, he firmly emphasized that it is my responsibility as a member of the dominant culture to familiarize myself with their challenges and concerns. What Vance lobbied against, however, was the objectification of ethnic knowledge and how it could be used to categorize and accentuate difference, resulting in communication breaks, not helpful and ethical connections. Vance's ideas have been embraced by First Nations people in Canada and by several minority groups in Europe.

A sensitivity to issues of gender can also be seen in Vance's work. Rather than assume that societal expectations for women restrict choice, Vance takes a more collaborative approach where he asks clients to pay attention to the kinds of scripts they may have taken up. As you will read, he respectfully suggests that women join together, so that experiences that may seem "natural" or "normal" can be re-examined and understood as merely social constructions that privilege some people in society and not others.

Vance mentions several aspects of human capacity that are required in order to work within the spaces between different perspectives, but one in particular deserves further mention. Counsellors, he argues, must be willing to be self-reflective. Conscious awareness on the part of the counsellor is not an end state but a constant process that requires a disciplined approach to reflecting on taken-for-granted assumptions. This kind of awareness differs from an awakened mind in the Buddhist sense but involves a full appreciation of the suffering that people endure due to discrimination and ignorance. It behooves the mindful counsellor, he points out, never to lose sight of the difficulties certain members of society endure because of the hegemonic practices used by those in positions of power.

Disciplined attentiveness to such issues requires an ongoing commitment to move outside one's level of comfort in order to understand relations of power and domination. Counsellors need to avoid making judgments about how people "should" live their lives; however, studying philosophical ideas about what constitutes the "good" is a positive step toward practising ethically. Without being what Vance describes as moralistic, it is possible for helping professionals to develop ethical decision making that can bring codes of ethics to life. Reading in philosophy and literature can foster skills in critical reflection needed to be a mindful and ethical practitioner. Throughout this book, Vance attends to several ethical issues in sensitive and respectful ways.

Vance addresses certain critiques of Western psychology when he deconstructs some of the legacy that has been left to us by the kind of behaviourism that dominated psychology in the mid-1950s. Such a perspective is no longer useful, he argues, in today's world of multiplicity, saturation, and complexity. Vance believed we would all be better off if we could move away from thinking of people as constellations of traits and factors and think instead of each person as occupying a unique life-space. Concepts such as narrative, symbolic co-ordination, self-authoring, life-space, attitudes, ethical assumptions, frames of mind, and meaning-making are likely to be more useful for understanding human actions and the dynamics of social life than concepts such as personality variables, traits, classifications, and behaviour, both normal and abnormal. Within a person's life-space, it is possible to explore thoughts, feelings, and actions within a linguistic framework and not get sidetracked by thinking only of visible behaviours. We could speak of local and cultural knowledge and how such knowledge shapes people's attitudes toward living. In an article about the role of counselling in society, Vance stated: "When counselling is defined by a cultural practice, the skilful counsellor practices a craft which is constituted of astute folk wisdom, locally relevant knowledge and culturally sensible communication. Counselling as a cultural practice is inclined to holism rather than compartmentalism."[3] This holistic, life-space approach has refreshing possibilities, particularly when contrasted with traditional cognitive and behavioural approaches.

---

3. Peavy, V. (1996). Counselling as a culture of healing. *British Journal of Guidance and Counselling, 24*(1), pp. 141-150.

Who should read this book?

Although Vance has written this book for counsellors, it is important to note that he has adopted a broad definition of what constitutes counselling, making his work applicable to a variety of practitioners who attend to those experiencing life difficulties. Professionals such as nurses, clinical and counselling psychologists, child and youth care practitioners, social workers, and mediators all could use the ideas about relationship that Vance so clearly articulates. The notion of conceptual mapping that he describes in detail in this book, for example, could easily be adapted to workplace conflicts so that employees could understand better the life-space of their co-workers. Such deepened understandings could foster the negotiation of new, more harmonious relationships once the whole person, not just the workplace behaviours, is known. Although this kind of strategy requires a high level of trust, the possibilities for modified conceptual mapping activities between persons could be adapted to different contexts. Similarly, in heath care settings, nurse practitioners could use conceptual life-space mapping to understand the patient's meaning of an illness within the overall context of his or her life.

What Vance emphasizes is that when principles of compassion, cultural attunement, respect, authenticity, and disciplined mindfulness are incorporated into one's own counselling practice, whether when working one-to-one, in groups, or in community development, it is possible to create one's own activities for those people with whom one works. Vance always avoided using rigid counselling techniques and methods in his own practice and cautioned others to avoid contrived and inauthentic ways of relating. Beyond anything else, he believed that counselling activities must have integrity. Both counsellor and client need to agree that what is being proposed makes sense and is a useful thing to do in light of the issue at hand.

Vance strongly believed that the most precious gift a person can give, whether in a counselling relationship or everyday life, is the gift of presence. Such a gift can only be provided by showing a human face to another, not a remote, professional mask. Professionals, Vance believed, should never alienate themselves from the people they hope to serve. Deep and profound connections occur when people are willing to be known with all of their vulnerabilities, fears, and concerns, as well as their hopes and dreams. Vance's intention for this book is to speak openly and honestly to practitioners who engage in this difficult but rewarding work with others.

In this introduction, I have merely touched on some of the ideas that you are about to read. On a personal note, I want to conclude my comments by sharing a brief glimpse of the man behind the ideas. Vance was a caring, honest, and genuine person who worked diligently right up until the time of his death to make a difference in how people engage in professional helping. His hopeful, inspiring way of working with people comes from his experience of working through adverse experiences in his own life. It should come as no surprise that his own ability to transcend an impoverished beginning helped him to develop his resilient philosophy of life that frames his approach. All people, he stated, regardless of the individual constraints and challenges they have to endure, have the opportunity to construct a meaningful, productive, and "good" life for themselves—it's just that some people need help in realizing the potential of their lives. Dialogical conversations are the best methods that people have invented for negotiating with each other, the best methods they have for thinking together and building together and for showing respect to each other. Counselling, at its best, is dialogue in the service of human need. Much can be learned about human experience by paying attention to the ways in which we converse with each other in formal helping relationships and in the informal dialogues we have in everyday life. Vance's visionary and hopeful leadership in the art and science of counselling will be greatly missed.

Dr. Marie L. Hoskins
Associate Faculty
School of Child and Youth Care
University of Victoria

Willow: (Auto)Biographical Reflections on Life and Theory[4]

The willow is a wonderful thing. You know why? Because it will live through the winter. It'll live through 60 degrees below zero. It will bend in the ice and it will come back up. It will live in the most amazingly difficult environments, and yet every spring it is so beautiful. I'm thinking of the little willows that live by streams. Bend but don't break. Stand there. Live in the harsh. Live in the sun.[5]

Self-metaphor by Vance Peavy

Aside from the standard biographical excerpt adorning the back cover of a book, rarely do we learn much about the life of authors of professional books. Occasionally, when very curious, we may attempt to create the story of an author based on clues we detect hidden in passages of theoretical discussion or brief anecdotes and illustrations. Yet we are primarily left to conjecture. So how might our understanding of our readings and our theory change, if we knew some of the life stories of those who write the books that influence our thoughts and our work?

These were some of my questions a number of years ago as I embarked on my doctoral research. At that time, I knew *of* Dr. Vance Peavy. I had read and admired his work, but we had never met. I had come to believe that counselling theories could mirror their authors' perceptions and interpretations of the world (Larsen, 1999).[6] Though he never stated so explicitly, I suspect that Vance

4. I gratefully acknowledge the Social Sciences and Humanities Research Council of Canada for supporting the foundational research for this biography.

5. All text in *italics* is the voice of Dr. Vance Peavy. All plain text is my voice, D. Larsen.

6. Larsen, D. (1999). Eclecticism: Psychological theories as interwoven stories. *International Journal of the Advancement of Counselling, 21*, pp. 69-83.

agreed. The metaphor shared above is Vance's and portrays much of his own life experience.[7] The additional biographical excerpts that follow are drawn from my research interviews with Vance, fascinating vignettes that I believe are engaging and lend fuller context for his theoretical work.

Riding the Range and Meeting a Reality

Fortune places us all in varying family circumstances, and we are left to make of them what we are able. Born in 1929, Vance grew up in the Colorado Rockies, where the family survived on subsistence ranching some forty long miles from the nearest town. When just a young boy, he worked the range, tending sheep in the hills above the family farm. As he did so, he dreamed of one day sparing his mother the desperate circumstances of their poor existence. For reprieve from the harsh realities of his childhood, he spun this dream into a beautiful fantasy—a fantasy of the flourishing ranch he would create for his mother and his family.

> *Well, when I was eleven years old, I was riding along through the sage brush. It was in the afternoon. It was hot. I was tired and was quite saddle sore by then ... . But in my mind, I'd been having my favourite fantasy. It was that one day, when I grew up, I would build a new ranch ... . It was a beautiful fantasy. I always felt so inspired that I was going to do this when I grew up.*

Unfortunately, this dream and the respite it provided could not last. With its passing, a crucial professional understanding developed. But this learning was not without heartache.

> *Then all of a sudden some shock went through me. I've often thought it's like the sky opened for a minute. I became conscious of myself as a young boy riding this horse*

---

7. All research information is shared with the prior written permission of the late Dr. Vance Peavy and the written permission of the executor of his estate, Judith Koltai-Peavy.

down the mountain and having a fantasy and that it wasn't
real and would not happen ... and I will never do those
things. This was an unrealizable fantasy. I felt this huge
sense of loss in me. I cried so much for a while after that.
But in the end it was a wonderful thing, because I became
aware of myself and I became aware of my mind—of when
it was fantasizing or not. I think that this insight has been
very instrumental when I work with other people. It has
made me very sensitive when I'm listening to their stories.
Are their stories connected to the realness of their life? Or
are their stories connected to their dreams? Are their sto-
ries, at this point, connected to innocent denial? Where
are they living in their stories? ... So this has had a funda-
mental influence on my practical conduct at counselling.

Experiences like this reflexively informed Vance's understanding of the relationship between realities, fantasies, and constructions. Other difficult experiences provided lessons as well. In the
end, Vance learned about choices in constructing a life—authoring
life in ways that sustain and that hold energy, imagination, and
spirit, often in the face of difficulty. The strength of his convictions was reinforced by the sheer magnitude of the deprivation he
had experienced as a child.

Desperation and Murderous Intent

Outward signs of destitution in Vance's childhood were pallid
reflections of the personal losses and poverty of relationships he
remembered as a child. When Vance spoke of seemingly unalter-
able realities, his words were born of raw experience. Terrorized
often by his drunken stepfather, as a young adolescent, Vance decided to take matters into his own hands. He needed the violence
to end. He needed to protect his mother and himself.

When I was 14 years old, things had gotten to be a worse
and worse situation between me and the man my mother
was married to. He drank heavily. He'd beat my mother,
choke her, and sometimes he'd beat me. One afternoon

he'd gone drinking to town, and I knew what he'd do to us when he returned ... so I got all the guns and put them away except for two and decided where I would situate myself and wait. He'd come out of the truck and that would be it.

So I waited and waited ... Suddenly, I was overcome by an anxiety attack, so I began to run. To show you how paranoid I was, I thought that I must get into the water and run so that he could not follow me. I ran about four miles down this little river.

Fortunately, I didn't do what I had in mind, or I would have gone to prison. I finally crawled out of the river and went to a house of a woman I called Auntie. She was a part native person. Anyway she took me in and gave me a bed. From that day forward, I was an independent, self-supporting person.

The devastation of Vance's childhood is undeniable. During our interview, I momentarily lost words as I took in his story. Yet his voice was strong and his understanding of the experience clear. From this radically life-altering episode came four key convictions that Vance would weave into his writing, his teaching, and his practice.

To begin, Vance claimed no self-righteous attitude toward those who are violent. He believed that given the right circumstance, we all hold violent, even murderous, potential within us. Further, he never entirely forgot the icy blade of fear. In counselling, Vance believed that it was important to remember what it was to live in a place of hopelessness. It was important to remember feeling mortal fear of another human being and the sinking sense that nothing could be done to change circumstances.

Given his own survival and the ways in which he grew to cherish his life, Vance also saw hope for others. According to him, *"No matter how bad the situation is, there is probably always something that can be done—some kind of alternative. Under the worst possible interpersonal human conditions, there is always something that can be done."* Profoundly affected by his experience of abuse, escape, and survival, Vance held an abiding belief in the strengths that others possess.

My experience also made me feel that in a lot of people there can be a pretty tough core there, and sometimes they need a little help to recognize that. I felt that my Auntie kind of held out her hand, but there was a tough core in me ... So it's very important in working with people to always be respectful. They may have a resource there.

Uncle John

With the love and support of his adoptive Auntie, Vance made his way in the world from the age of fourteen. Male role models were scarce. An American Ute Indian named John—*"Uncle John"* to Vance—took a special interest in Vance. Vance looked up to this large man both literally and figuratively, and Uncle John's gifts sustained Vance for a lifetime. He taught Vance to observe— to trust his intuition.

My only adult male role model or friend when I was grow- ing up was an Indian. He gave me the freedom to be silent. We used to ride together all the time. He spoke English well, but we never talked about Indians. He would just point out thing—mostly things about animals. He taught me to the see the signs and sounds of animals, like eagles and their language ... such rare knowledge. He was such a beautiful man. Several times he'd turn to me and say, "If you would close your mouth and use your eyes, you wouldn't be asking that question." He was right.

Inspiration

Vance's work shared much in common with aboriginal knowl- edge. At times, Vance spoke of honouring nature. He spoke of becoming aware of energy and inspiration. Just as Uncle John taught Vance the value of quietude, of listening to what is around as well as to the inspiration from within, Vance sought to provide the same to others. In his writing, his counselling, and his teaching, he sought to offer many of the gifts first introduced to him by Uncle John.

> *To me, inspiration is much more important than motivation, learning theory, or personality structure or whatever ... If I could give a gift to another person, I would give them this willingness to be inspired. I would give them the ability to observe carefully, to use their eyes and their ears, to be self-observing and observing of everything that is out there. I would give them a respect for and a love of language. By that, I mean I would include all kinds of symbolism—to take in, to give out, and to let language rise out of the silence that is within you. Every human being is filled with a well of silence. Most people try to cap that well or keep it filled up so that it doesn't bother them—but that's actually the source of their creativity.*

Daybreak

As I closed my research interviews with Vance, I asked him if he had a title for the narrative he had been creating with me. He listed two without hesitation: willow and daybreak. While his publications rarely speak directly of soul, Vance's understanding of spirituality was vital to sustaining his creative energy, his ideas, and his writing.

> *If I were to put a title to my story, you ask? Daybreak. Every day there is a dawn. And to see the dawn and to feel the dawn is to be inspired. And inspiration is to breathe in the fact of your life and the fact that you are in an eternal universe and that it is opening again with the sky. It's a most wonderful experience. It's the eternal mother opening the window to the day and there's such a rise of energy. I think that my whole life has been a kind of daybreak. When I walk as day breaks over the ocean, I feel filled with a radiant energy. I feel balanced in harmony. And for*

those moments, I am in harmony with all the four-leggeds and two-leggeds in the world.

A life without spirit is no life. I feel filled with creativity at those times. I don't try to think of anything. It is open. It's open to the power of my imagination and intelligence and the connectedness of myself with all that there is.

Nobility in Counselling

Just weeks before his unexpected death, Vance delivered a paper at the 2002 International Human Science Research Conference exploring the place of wisdom in therapy. For Vance, counselling was an inherently ethical activity replete with ongoing choices about who and how counsellors choose to be in conversation with clients. For this reason, he was fascinated by the profession, respectful of its power, and devoted to advancing constructivist theory and practice. I close with Vance's characterization of the counselling relationship:

Whatever this person brings, you face them and say, "Yes, I'm present with you; what is it? I'll be with you now for a while. Whatever it is." When counselling is like that, it's a fundamentally noble thing to be doing. There is nothing— there is no process in society, outside of maybe love relations—that has more nobility to it than that.

Denise J. Larsen, Ph.D.
Assistant Professor, Counselling Psychology
Department of Educational Psychology
University of Alberta
and
Director of Research, Hope Foundation of Alberta

xxiii

Chapter 1: Introduction

Over the past four decades I have organized, defined, and published numerous papers and several books on the SocioDynamic perspective and counselling practices based on this perspective.[1] This book is a guidebook for practising counsellors, psychologists, and other helping professionals who wish to familiarize themselves with the SocioDynamic perspective and counselling ideas and practices.

This is *not* a book about other books. I do not inundate the reader with a "sea of names" by making constant references to the research and ideas of other counselling specialists. Likewise, I make only limited references to intellectual sources upon which I rely. The SocioDynamic perspective presented in this book is composed of 1) a *philosophy of helping* and 2) *practical methods of counselling* informed by and informing the philosophy. While the second chapter deals directly with the philosophy of helping, there are philosophical ideas throughout the book, most of which are part of the SocioDynamic philosophy of helping.

Throughout this book I use the terms *helper* and *counsellor*, and *counselling* and *helping* interchangeably. I also use the term *help-seeker*[2] instead of "client" or "patient" and the terms *counselling conversation* or *dialogue* instead of "interview."

Readers will recognize similarities between elements of this perspective and other helping approaches, especially person-centred counselling, systems theory-based therapy and counselling, narrative-based approaches to helping, and activity-based counselling. Of course, nothing is ever completely new—we always work from the shoulders of others who have gone before us.

There also are clear differences between SocioDynamic counselling[3] and other forms of counselling. One important difference is that the SocioDynamic perspective uses a vocabulary that neither psychopathologizes[4] people and their actions, nor objectifies[5] them through classification and diagnosis.[6]

Another important difference between SocioDynamic counselling and many other conventional counselling models is that

1

the SocioDynamic perspective does not invoke the metaphor of "curing." It is not a form of "therapy." Instead of therapy, the SocioDynamic counselling process is viewed as a learning process, a process of co-construction, a life-planning process, and a means of extending perspective, choice, capacity, opportunity, and thus, personal freedom. For the reader with an academic interest, I have written a bibliographic essay[7] that identifies many of the ideas and intellectual sources upon which the SocioDynamic perspective is based.

The SocioDynamic Perspective: A Way of Thinking

In this book I convey a way of thinking—about how people function and try to solve practical problems in contemporary social life, and what it means to help others through the process of counselling. I begin by presenting a *philosophy of helping* that is designed with post-industrial social life in mind. I am concerned with *ideas* about people, society, how to live successfully, and about *ideas* that can inform acts of helping. One of the secrets of good helping is the recognition that ideas guide actions in life. The capacity to *reflect* on ideas and their meanings and to reflect on one's experience, feelings, assumptions, and perceptions, makes ideas even more important as guideposts in everyday living.

As beings-in-the-world, we live in an environment of ideas. Ideas and perspectives are the tools that enable us to communicate, relate, plan, choose, construct, get stuck, overcome constraints, create freedoms, and try to move on in life. As we try to move on, we *articulate* our consciousness of the existential realities of our present, *remember* our past, and *invent* new futures. What we can articulate and remember from our experience and store of ideas and invent through the use of perception and imagination provides us with the materials-at-hand with which to construct and co-construct our lives.

In our environment of ideas, *ethical* ideas are especially important for responding to the questions "How *should* I live my life?" "What are *good* actions to take?" and "What *should* I do next?"

2

Some ideas are *instrumental*. They can inform us on *what* to do and *how* to do it. Other ideas are *ethical*. They inform us about what *ought to* be done—what is *good* to do or to be. It is very helpful to learn how to evaluate ideas and their meanings in the context of everyday living. I believe that the process of counselling is qualitatively improved when meanings, ideas, perspectives, experience, assumptions, values, intentions, and actions are articulated, critically evaluated, and understood *within the context of the individual help-seeker's life-space.*

SocioDynamic Counselling: An Ethical Practice
We can think of a "good" life or "good" ends in life or even of being a "good" person. There are many differences in the way the ethical idea of "good" is interpreted. I can only say what I mean by "good" within the SocioDynamic framework.

Within this perspective, helping others who are in need is "good." This might be called the altruistic ethic. It is especially good to help others in ways that alleviate their problems, while strengthening their self-esteem and their capacities to choose and act self-responsibly. The counsellor who is able to help others in a way that does not interfere, disrespect, or demean the self-identity of the other, but instead affirms and strengthens the capacity of the other to think, feel, and act in self-dependent ways, is engaging in counselling as an ethical practice.

So, what do I mean by "good" with reference to helping? What are the *good ends* and good *ways of being* that make counselling ethical? Counselling as an ethical practice embodies good ends and is a good way of being a counsellor when it can be described as follows:

Helping is good when it
- Reduces pain and suffering,
- Reduces cruelty,
- Improves interpersonal understanding,
- Assists another to articulate his or her own life experience,
- Results in strengthened self-esteem on the part of the help-seeker,

3

- Helps an individual to move toward goals of his or her own choosing—so long as those goals do not bring harm to others,
- Supports the help-seeker to increase his or her capacity to perform needed skills for success in social life,
- Provides social support and emotional safety,
- Facilitates the self-responsible participation of help-seekers in social life,
- Results in the help-seeker achieving more adequate material conditions for his or her own life,
- Increases the range of choices an individual can make within the spectrum of available opportunities, and
- Reduces the need for its own existence.

To claim that we live in an ethical environment does *not* mean that a person knows with absolute certainty what is good to do, or how to be good in every instance of decision and action. It does mean, however, that we humans are ethical creatures. We make claims, justify, decide, prefer, feel, and think about the relationship between means and ends in our daily lives. It is the task of counsellors to remain alert to the ethical question "What *should* I do?" as well as the more utilitarian questions "What can I do and how *can* I do this?"

SocioDynamic Counselling: A Form of "Language Game"
From the SocioDynamic perspective, counselling is primarily a "language game." To counsel in a particular way is to use a certain vocabulary that guides, constrains, and inspires counsellors to think and act in certain ways and not in others. The selves that we are, the relationships in which we participate, and the social spaces that we inhabit are co-constructed using symbolic-linguistic means. To utter a sentence, to employ a metaphor, to use a certain tone of voice, to speak a word—each of these linguistic actions and countless others are *moves* in the language game of meaning construction and symbolic interaction.

Human life is *linguistic* life. In everyday living, including counselling, the basic problem-solving tools are language (mental) tools.

4

The counselling process and any solutions produced by counselling are *interactional achievements* that have been interpersonally negotiated by the helper and help-seeker. The counselling relationship is inevitably co-produced by helper and help-seeker through their linguistic and emotional responsiveness and negotiation with each other.

A New Vocabulary for Counselling

Conventional forms of counselling, such as cognitive-behavioural, psychodynamic, and humanistic counselling, have vocabularies that are well established. Of course these forms of counselling have merit. A large body of research supports the value of counselling—no matter which counselling method is being applied.

However, traditional forms of counselling do suffer from adherence to long-standing vocabularies that are becoming obsolete and, to a degree, have outlived their usefulness. This is due, in part, to the fact that most conventional forms of counselling were developed during the factory age and under the influence of positivist social science. The factory age is ending, and an "industrial mind" is no longer adequate to understand contemporary social life. Positivist vocabularies used in social science are now being eclipsed by more recent vocabularies, such as those of constructivism, feminism, narrative, systems theory, chaos and complexity theory, ethnography, and symbolic interactionism.

Society is changing. When societies change, people change, and the vocabularies they use to describe their life experience also change. In order to maintain its relevance and meet the needs of help-seekers in contemporary society, counselling must also change—in terms of both vocabulary and methods of practice.

In this introduction to SocioDynamic counselling, I am not trying to prove that "My way is better than your way." Rather, my approach is to describe and re-describe the ideas that make up the SocioDynamic perspective for counselling. In this way, I hope to create a new vocabulary for counselling—a new configuration of meanings or a new "language game" that will tempt rising generations of counsellors to adopt it. These new meanings and language, in turn, can lead to inventing new forms of non-linguistic behaviour and new forms of activity that will prove helpful to people in resolving practical problems in their everyday lives.

The SocioDynamic perspective says: "Here is another way. Try thinking in this way and see what doing so will do for you." With any way of thinking, one should pose the question "What does this way of thinking do? What is the influence of this way of thinking on the practices in my life?" The SocioDynamic perspective suggests that it is a good idea to stop doing "the same old things in counselling" and start doing something else instead. The unpredictability and fluidity[8] of contemporary society requires new forms of counselling.

In recent decades, narrative[9] and systems-based counselling models[10] and philosophical[11] or wisdom-based forms of counselling have emerged. They tend to be informed by postmodern[12] ways of thinking. These use evolving *new* vocabularies of what it means to help others. SocioDynamic counselling takes its place beside, but is not identical with, these newer vocabularies of helping.

In creating a new counselling vocabulary, we can draw on philosophical ideas, literary forms, and socio-cultural studies to inform the practice of counselling. We can use metaphors of "creating possibility," "expanding choices," "capacity building," and "personal freedom," rather than metaphors of "finding deficiency," "pathology," and "adjustment." Of course, every human being is also psychological. We can continue to borrow ideas from psychology, sociology, and education to construct counselling practice that is in keeping with societal change.

The SocioDynamic perspective is a *spanning perspective*. Ideas from different disciplines are placed into mutual relations with one another without losing the integrity of each idea. The vocabulary of SocioDynamic perspective is not dominated by a single discipline.

An Ironic Frame of Mind for Counsellors

The SocioDynamic frame of mind favours irony and a certain caution toward literalness when trying to understand and describe what is going on in human actions and predicaments. An ironist's method of thinking and expression is dialectical and tries to play off the new against the old, using metaphor, figurative language, and humour to unmask fossilized ideas and perspectives that constrain forward movement in life.

The ironic mind is in contrast to the factory-mind that thrives on literalness, instrumental thinking, classification, objectivity, and efficiency. Factory-minded literalness reflects a kind of certainty that things can be measured and evaluated according to pre-set criteria. An ironist is not so sure about this and is open to the possibility that criteria are created or emerge as processes unfold. The ironic method prefers to present old ideas and words in new ways. By being introduced to brand-new words and ideas, people may no longer ask questions and interpret the world using the old ideas and words. *Things do not have to be the way they usually are or always have been.*

The counsellor-as-ironist hopes for the opportunity to construct a good life for him or her self and a chance to use the counselling process to help others do likewise. He or she does this through intelligent and creative use of ideas, words, and language to describe and re-describe and by remaining open to the emergent nature of the life process.

Where Is the Problem?

SocioDynamic Counselling has a different point of departure than many other models of helping. Instead of being predominantly psyche-centred and looking for what is wrong inside of the person or in the person's behaviour, the SocioDynamic approach is interested in two aspects of helping: first, the dynamics of relationships and contexts, and second, perspectives, or ways of thinking and feeling.

As a method, SocioDynamic counselling is designed to
1. Assist people to recognize their achievements, personal strengths, and potentialities;
2. Support and guide people in developing their capacities so that they are enabled to move forward in life under the expanded influence of the choices, abilities, and goals they

value. The SocioDynamic impulse is to develop "guidance from the inside."[13]

3. Place more emphasis on context, sociality, and the co-construction of social and personal realities. Problems are often not located "inside" the minds and personalities of individuals. Instead, they are located in the context, "between people," or between people and the contexts in which they live.

   Problems are often the consequence of failure in interpersonal communication, breakdown or misuse of relationships, or lack of fit between individual desire and contextual opportunity. The person is viewed as a *social actor* and *moral agent*. The terms *act*, *action*, and *activity* are used in preference to the term *behaviour*. The self of a person is socially constructed using language and regarded as a complex organized system of meanings, which are used by the person-as-agent to negotiate with others, interpret the world, and guide actions.

4. Use descriptions of meaning and experience as the primary source of motivation. Ideas, perspectives, and meanings profoundly influence our actions and form the basis for negotiating and communicating with others.

Thinking in the Constructive Present

The SocioDynamic process can be enormously empowering for both helpers and help-seekers. To work from positions of strength-building, creativity, and cooperative engagement is an inspiring and liberating process. Persons who have been conditioned to think of themselves as incapable, disadvantaged, outcast, or marginalized can be amazed when they are made aware of their own strengths and have these strengths confirmed though meaningful dialogue and activity.

Clarification of possibilities and opportunities opens windows of hope. The counselling process should aid people to re-frame their self-identities, validate what they have already done and can do, and open cultural paths for building new capacities. This process facilitates a turn from self-perspectives of passivity or helplessness to a view of self as a *resilient survivor*. Instead of construing themselves as trapped and helpless, help-seekers can construct new understandings of self as capable and creative and as a rich source of valuable personal resources. If you think you can't, you can't. If you think you can, you can.

People who are living in poverty or marginalized for whatever reasons, or who have become trapped in an internal prison of restrictive and paralyzing constructs, can come to realize that just having survived is evidence of their resilience. Without doubt, poverty, oppression, marginality, and lack of opportunity are cruel and demeaning conditions. However, having been dealt a bad hand in life does not mean that the game is over. The lives of individuals such as Viktor Frankl[14] demonstrate that even when living with the indescribable horror of a concentration camp, survival depends on a resilient "will to meaning" and a belief that "I *can* survive." Even under the worst imaginable conditions of existence, meaning and ideas are of value.

To assist help-seekers invent "escape routes" from undesirable conditions, counsellors can use the *constructive present* to help others to visualize and construct a better future. A constructive present combines three elements: 1) the existential realities that exist in the present, 2) possibilities and imagined futures, 3) while at the same time resisting unrealistic fantasizing and self-descriptions of helplessness.

SocioDynamic counselling assists individuals to move forward in life along capacity-developing pathways. Helping efforts are based on what can be constructed, learned, and implemented, not on what is wrong, deficient, or impossible. This attitude of "thinking in the constructive present" underlies all SocioDynamic helping strategies.

The Test of Experience

The fruitfulness of each idea and description of practice included in this book has been evaluated by both helpers and help-seekers, using the test of actual experience. No claim is made that these practices are more effective than others. Instead, the reader is invited to reflect on the SocioDynamic perspective and ideas and to try out the counselling practices presented in this book. Then, using practice and reflected-on-experience, both helpers and help-seekers will be in a position to decide on the value of the SocioDynamic ideas and practices. The test of efficacy is in the doing, and in reflection on the experience of doing, not in theory *about* doing.

Based on decades of study and practice, I have found the ideas and practices described in the following pages to be very helpful to me in the various roles I have assumed in my professional journey as counsellor, psychologist, teacher, manager, therapist, supervisor, colleague, and reflective thinker.

How the Rest of this Book Is Organized

Chapter 2 describes the SocioDynamic philosophy of helping. This chapter is intended to give readers a sense of what it means to help from the SocioDynamic perspective. It also introduces the vocabulary and some of the main ideas of SocioDynamic helping.

Chapter 3 describes the main practices of SocioDynamic counselling, including both guiding ideas and practical procedures.

Chapter 4 provides a narrative description of a counselling scenario with a 17-year-old male. It includes commentaries on many of the important ideas of SocioDynamic counselling as illustrated by the interaction of helper and help-seeker in the scenario.

The final section of the book contains the endnotes, including references.

I believe that the book in its entirety describes the *counsellor attitude* proposed for SocioDynamic helping. In many instances, the *counsellor's attitude*, including his or her frame of mind, perspectives, and world view, will exert more influence on the counselling process and on the help-seeker than any other factor.

To conclude this introduction, I have chosen two quotations. The first is from Richard Rorty:

All humans carry about a set of words which they employ to justify their actions, their beliefs, and their lives .... They are the words in which we tell, sometimes prospectively and sometimes retrospectively, the story of our lives. [15]

The second is from Ludwig Wittgenstein's *vermischte Bemerkungen*:

> *Getting hold of the difficulty* deep down *is what is hard. Because it is grasped near the surface, it simply remains the difficulty it was. It has to be pulled out by the roots, and that involves* beginning to think in a new way. *The change is as decisive, for example, as that from the alchemical to the chemical way of thinking. The new way of thinking is what is so hard to establish.*
>
> *Once the new way of thinking has been established, many of the old problems vanish; indeed they become hard to recapture, for they go with our way of expressing ourselves. If we clothe ourselves in a new form of expression, the old problems are discarded along with the old garment.* [16]

Words are tools for constructing and authoring a life. It makes a difference what vocabulary you choose your tools from.

Chapter 2: The SocioDynamic Philosophy of Helping

Limitations of Industrial-Age Models of Counselling

A criticism sometimes made of industrial-age forms of counselling is an over-emphasis on methods for changing personality and on behavioural adjustment, together with neglect of the importance of language, meaning, and wholeness.[17] In order to implement these goals, counsellors and other helping professionals are taught an array of "techniques" with which to assess and diagnose and "interventions" designed to change behaviour and personality variables.

From a SocioDynamic perspective, there are several difficulties with this prominent emphasis on techniques and interventions for changing behaviour. First, post-Kuhnian[18] thinking in the social sciences, as well as writings by post-analytical philosophy scholars such as Charles Taylor,[19] Richard Rorty,[20] and Alasdair MacIntyre,[21] emphasize the need for new vocabularies for understanding how self, identity, and social life develop and function. The very conception of "self" has changed in recent decades. There is a significant movement from a theory of the "psychometric" self composed of variables to a "narrated" self constructed by means of stories and meanings.

Second, some writers and researchers on counselling are inclined to argue that counselling is based on scientific research and that counsellors should be regarded as scientist-practitioners. I believe that these arguments are pretentious.[22] For the most part, the efforts to predict individual behaviour reliably have not been successful. Further, after more than a century of research, the efforts of psychological science to provide universal laws about human behaviour have not been impressive.

A more general intellectualism in the profession of counselling is needed. There should be a conversation among various disciplines—literary theory, philosophy, anthropology, sociology, psychology, socio-cultural studies, communication science, and

13

education—about how best to understand human actions and provide useful counselling methods and strategies. It is probably better to regard counselling as a primarily culturally based practice, not as a scientifically justified practice.

Counselling benefits more from strategies of "best guess," based on the interdisciplinary pooling of ideas and knowledge, than from efforts to predict and explain human behaviour by scientific findings. By this, I do not mean that scientific evidence should be disregarded, rather that the voice of science, and especially psychological science, should be one of many used to inform counselling.

The exclusive domination of counselling by the science of psychology is not adequate today. Of course, an individual is psychological, and social, and cultural, and self-authoring. Counsellors, and other helping professionals, need *multiple* lenses for observing and understanding people and their thoughts, feelings, and actions.

Concepts such as narrative, symbolic co-construction, self-authoring, life-space, perspective, attitude, ethical assumptions, frames of mind, and meaning making are likely to be more useful for understanding human actions and the dynamics of social life than concepts such as personality variables, traits, classifications, and behaviour—both normal and abnormal.

While not universal, there is a definite shift from a paradigmatic view of people as "behaviour emitters" and "information processors" to the perspective that people are "storytellers" and "meaning makers" and co-constructive "world makers." Increasingly, there is recognition that ideas, mental perspectives, ethical reasoning, and meaning give momentum and direction to action. In this perspective, human action is motivated by the desire for, and the creation of, meaning. Another way of saying this is that all deliberate human action is *perspectival*. How we act and interact in any situation depends upon the perspectives we bring to that situation.

In an effort to transcend positivist, industrial-age formulations for counselling, the SocioDynamic perspective uses such concepts as meaning making, storytelling, narrated self, joint action, guided participation, life-space, mindful problem solving, and language tools. The emphasis in counselling is shifted from behaviour technology to symbolic construction and from personality structure to contextualized formation of self-identity and perspectives. Moreover, attention is directed toward the application of ethical, meaningful, and pragmatically useful ideas in counselling and away from exclusive reliance on concepts of behaviour and behaviour change.

Third, most conventional forms of counselling are marked by an absence of a philosophy of helping upon which to base counselling practice. Most counselling approaches focus primarily on "technical" competencies and prescriptive interventions. In the literature of industrial-age counselling, philosophical ideas either are missing or are derided as mere ruminations and examples of fuzzy thinking. In contrast, the SocioDynamic perspective accords to philosophical thinking a legitimate and important status.

The Importance of Philosophical Ideas in Counselling

Most counselling methods ask counsellors to work from the instrumental questions: "What *can* a helper do that is helpful to a particular help-seeker in a particular context, and what *can* the help-seeker do or learn to do that will be self-helpful?" These questions refer to the helping and problem-solving functions and activities that *can* be performed, given opportunity to do so. Naturally, they are important questions and much of counselling is an attempt to answer them.

Equally important questions for both helper and help-seeker are the questions: "What *should* I do? How *should* I proceed in my life to resolve this issue? How *should* I live my life?" These are philosophical questions that imply the need for ethical reasoning and decision making and point to the importance of recognizing that individuals are *moral agents* who make decisions and act on the basis of reasons that make sense and have meaning for them.

People thus ask ethical questions and decide what to do about their concerns on the basis of *both* instrumental reasoning and moral/ethical reasoning. Our value as counsellors is largely our consciousness of how we stand before other fellow human beings.

15

What *should* we do for others, as well as what *can* we do to support others in their efforts to move forward in life as self-responsible actors?

From a SocioDynamic perspective, an important function of counselling and counsellors is to assist others (and themselves) to articulate, evaluate, and create ideas about how to live their lives. Counselling, from a SocioDynamic perspective, is guided by "good ideas" about living as well as being guided by instrumental means of achieving goals. We are surrounded by, and living in, an environment of ideas—some provide ethical guidance and others do not. The actions of both saints and despots are driven by ideas, and both compassion and cruelty are rooted in ideas about how one should live.

In modern, industrial societies there has been a proliferation of formulas for being efficient, quick, and effective and doing the most at the least cost. This "technique-driven and time-starved" attitude unfortunately often leads to the devaluing of reflective thinking, of wise decision making, and of ideas about how to lead a "good" life. Doing good and being good are forsaken for the goals of being efficient, effective, and quick—attitudes that most social commentators agree lead to a life of stress and anxiety. The question is, what else can we do?

I wish to clearly distinguish between "moralistic" attitudes, which I am not advocating, and "ethical reasoning," which I am advocating. The term *moralistic* conjures up closed-mindedness, judgmentalism, prejudice, self-righteousness, absolutism, and fundamentalist thinking. My claim is that humans are ethical creatures and that for better or worse, we live in an ethical environment.

To take a responsible position in an ethical environment means having a desire to understand feelings, values, motivations, and ideas that move both ourselves and others. It means placing a strong value on self-knowledge and relationships. It means not acting in harmful or cruel ways toward others. It requires that we examine and evaluate ideas in terms of their power to promote responsibility as individuals and in relationships with others. Generally, we need to be guided in everyday life by ethical ideas in terms of their "goodness."

16

Unfortunately, ethical decisions and conflicts cannot really be settled in counselling situations by referring to codes of ethics or a list of ethical do's and don'ts. From a SocioDynamic point of view, ethicality rests on critical thinking, dialogue, reality negotiation, relationship, and willingness to acknowledge multiple realities and shades of meaning. For the most part, we cannot settle ethical contradictions by reading from an ethics cookbook of rules, judicial procedures, authoritative truth, and sanctions.

Ethics is not a special set of judgements only to be applied when some rule has been ignored or overlooked. We are engaged in ethical decision making all the time, in all aspects of our daily life.

To engage in ethical thinking is often disturbing. Making ethical distinctions about what should be done is neither easy nor always calming. One must be able to appreciate shades of meaning, be willing to negotiate multiple meanings embedded in existential situations, clarify ethical reasons, make decisions, and act in self-responsible ways. Ethical thinking invokes attention to relationships, use of language, context, cultural customs, responsibility as an individual, and social responsibility. Ethical thinking requires that we pay attention to the power of ideas as well as actions.

Counsellors hear countless stories from help-seekers about ethical issues, about what should be done in the name of self-affirmation, or constructive relations, or even in the name of survival as a person with dignity. Placing value on self-knowledge, assuming personal and social responsibility, engaging in dialogue, taking pride in supporting good in social life, encouraging critical thinking, and showing respect for the views of those different from ourselves are some guidelines for counsellors making ethical decisions and conducting themselves ethically.

Ideas for Guiding the Process of Counselling

This section describes thirteen ideas that are central to the SocioDynamic philosophy of helping. My claim is that each idea, when properly implemented in counselling practice, will make counselling a more valuable practice. How these ideas are used in practice is contingent on what each situation uniquely calls for.

None of the ideas is always applicable, nor is any single idea always the best guide in every counselling situation.

The ideas that follow come from a range of thinking modes—philosophical, literary, psychological, linguistic, and socio-cultural—as well as from that boundless sea of notions referred to as cultural common sense. I try to present each idea in a manner that makes clear to the reader its potential usefulness as a guiding idea in helping. I make no claim about the relative importance of the concepts. Taken together, they indicate what is meant by a "SocioDynamic philosophy of helping."

Counselling and Social Capital Are Interdependent

There is no question that economic and political capital in contemporary society is important. Emphasis on the significance of commerce, finance, profit making, markets and production is everywhere. Just as important, but not so strongly emphasized in many societies, is *social capital*; those policies, programs and practices designed to support the well-being and dignity of people as individuals, as family members, and as community participants. People, their social and personal well being, their skills and talents, as well as social policies and social support systems constitute *social capital*.

Democratic societies include the belief that every individual has civil rights and is entitled to the opportunity to develop a life worth living. Although many people are frustrated in their efforts to achieve it, *self-fulfilment* remains a primary and important goal for members of contemporary societies. Opportunities for self-fulfilment are a key component of the social capital of a society. Persons desiring self-fulfilment are frustrated by many factors: poverty, inadequate access to health, imprisonment, lack of education, marginalization and prejudice based on ethnicity, race and ability, gender inequity, inadequate pension systems and warehousing of the elderly, for example.

Social capital is developed principally through policy, social structuring, and legislation. However, as long as social capital is not supported and adequately provided for, individuals are left to their own resources to try and find escape routes from deprivation

18

and marginalization, and must rely on do-it-yourself methods of gaining self-fulfilment.

Finding fulfilment has become a do-it-yourself process as social support systems have shrunk and traditional forms of guidance (family, church, elders, community) are altered and weakened in their influence. Counselling is one of the few remaining activities that can help individuals to find and construct escape routes from unemployment, poverty, lack of capacity, cultural confusion, or other forms of marginalization and that can support people in their quest for self-fulfilment.

Counselling is a process specifically designed for one person (counsellor) to assist another person (help-seeker) with concrete problems in daily living. Counselling, as a one-to-one helping process, is one of the few existential encounters left in contemporary society where genuine listening can occur and where the particular concerns of the individual can be brought forward and problems worked through. While counselling cannot change social structures or social policies, counselling is a fundamental means of developing social capital on the level of interpersonal and individual social life.

The Counsellor Should Present a Human Face

From a SocioDynamic perspective, counsellors should present a *human face* in their meetings with help-seekers. Research by Goffman[23] into the dynamics of everyday life provides convincing arguments that an individual engages in "self-presentation" strategies in every situation. The strategies vary with the self-presentation ability of the individual, the impression he or she wishes to make on others, and the demands of specific situations, especially in terms of power and control.

The socialization of helping professionals typically orients them toward self-presentation strategies, such as presenting the self as

1. An expert, that is, "one who knows best,"
2. Objective and free from personal bias,
3. "In control,"
4. An official,

19

5. Spokesman for approved standards of behaviour, or
6. A scientifically or technically informed professional.

Each of these self-presentation strategies positions the helper in a superior status to the help-seeker. Moreover, these presentation strategies operate to elevate the helper into a "distanced," objective position with regard to both help-seekers and everyday social life. One effect of each of these self-presentation strategies is alienation of the helper from the help-seeker.

In contrast with self-presentation strategies designed to give the helper a position of authority with regard to help-seekers, the SocioDynamic philosophy of helping advocates that a counselling session is a genuine human meeting between two persons, each of whom is entitled to respect. Any positioning of authority should be because of knowledge and not status, role, or location in social life. The point is not that helper and help-seeker are equals, but that their differences are to be respected and not to be used as a method for exerting personal power and gaining control of the other.

Martin Buber[24] wrote that a compassionate human face, when unadorned by pretence, role, or assumption of superiority, offers more hope to another than the most sophisticated psychological techniques. The SocioDynamic ideal is to seek a working partnership between helper and help-seeker on the basis of common humanity and respect for difference. Both helper and help-seeker have important contributions to make to the counselling relationship.

The counselling relationship is not that of one-who-knows and one-who-does-not-know, but rather a relationship of negotiation and co-participation. I do not claim that helper and help-seeker are "equal" in terms of power or knowledge. I *do* claim that each can make important contributions to the counselling process. Further, the counselling process is *more valuable* when both counsellor and help-seeker offer the other respect as a person and respect for what each can contribute to the process of counselling.

When meeting with help-seekers, it is quite common for helpers to present themselves as *officials* of an institution, representing the institution, and sometimes acting as controller, or even performing surveillance. At other times, the counsellor presents a face as a *bureaucrat* whose job it is to explain rules and policies. Yet other counsellors define themselves as *objective data sources*, whose job is that of presenting help-seekers with realistic and accurate information. These self-presentations are tied closely to institutionally defined roles. Such personas are nearly always characterized by some degree of "objectivity," "distancing," "secrecy," "expertise," and "impersonality." They may convey "suspiciousness," "distrust," "an authoritarian attitude of 'knowing best' ," and even prejudicial attitudes based on race, ethnicity, gender, or social class.

However, when *facing another as a fellow human*, it is very difficult to disavow a sense of responsibility for that aspect of the other's life that comes under discussion in the counselling conversation. A "human" face smiles, shows interest, offers respect, reflects self-knowledge that enables dialogue, and conveys a certain openness to the giving and receiving of human feeling. A human face, devoid of mask, reveals the "who" of the helper and gives clues to the other person about the degree to which the helper can be counted on to care and help.

To Help Others Is an Ethical Good

To act in helpful ways toward others is an ethical "good" independent of any doctrine. Helpers and help-seekers belong to a common humanity, regardless of status, skin colour, age, gender, or other differentiating features. There is no known culture that does not have the role of personal helper—counsellor, priest, shaman, medicine woman, social worker, mentor, elder, helper, therapist. Designations of helping roles vary from culture to culture. The specific function and form that helping takes are always culturally defined.

The purposes of helping are many: reducing suffering, supporting personal freedom and autonomy, aiding others to overcome oppressive conditions and surmount barriers to successful living, helping others to make decisions, assisting with practical life planning, solving concrete problems in everyday living, fostering capacity,

21

validating personal experience, creating new perspectives, strengthening personal identity, and harmonizing relations.

Genuine helping should be offered under conditions of respect for the integrity and uniqueness of the help-seeker. Except under exceptional conditions of emergency or imminent harm, offers of help should be free from intrusion, coercion, interventionism, and imposition.

In modern societies, helping has become a commodity, and many people receive payment for helping others. However, genuine helping, even as a commodity, can still be consistent with spiritual and ethical traditions of care and compassion, love and peace. This is true so long as the purpose of helping is to support the dignity, choices, goals, and capacity of the individual who seeks help and who wishes to engage in constructive participation in social life.

From the SocioDynamic perspective, counselling is one of the most important activities in contemporary social life. In post-industrial societies, there are few possibilities for having a conversation where the other is a good and patient listener who helps to articulate personal experience and who joins as a partner in problem-solving and life-planning dialogue. In this context, the genuine counselling meeting is potentially of enormous importance to those individuals who face challenges in everyday life for which they cannot find or create a satisfactory resolution on their own.

Counselling can be a safe, sheltering place to pause momentarily in the hurly-burly of everyday life. Here one can "take stock" through conversation with a helpful person who is interested, supportive, and resourceful. Here one can realize desire and gather strength to face difficulties and proceed with new and renewed efforts to navigate successfully pathways in cultural life.

As a temporary sanctuary and workshop for life planning and rethinking personal experience, SocioDynamic counselling is designed to provide some or all of the following ten resources:

1. Assistance in articulating life-space experience and meaning;
2. Emotional-social support, trustworthiness, and compassion;

3. Dialogical communication, including patient, non-intrusive listening and intelligent conversation;
4. Access to information, networks, and other resources;
5. Life planning and lifestyle review and revision;
6. Better-than-ordinary evaluation of ideas and perspectives;
7. Focussed, mindful problem solving;
8. Cooperation in terms of shared intelligence, imagination, and ideas for overcoming personal difficulties and obstacles to successful living in everyday life;
9. Recognition of uniqueness and diversity, especially in terms of cultural experience and membership; and
10. Conditions of learning that support choice and capacity building.

Of course, the degree to which these ten features of SocioDynamic counselling prevail in any particular counselling encounter will vary along many dimensions. Especially influential will be the cultural characteristics, attitudes, and knowledge that the helper and help-seeker possess. Helping that is sensible in one cultural context is not necessarily useful in another.

Other factors that can greatly influence the counselling encounter are 1) the needs and expectations of the help-seeker; 2) the overall competency, attitude toward helping, and wisdom of the counsellor; and 3) the institutionally defined purpose of the counselling offered in a specific context.

Counselling Should Promote Personal Freedom

In *Development as Freedom*, Amartya Sen,[25] winner of the 1998 Nobel Prize in economic science, presents a careful analysis of the relation between economic resources in society and the ability of people to live as they would like. He is concerned with both the development of society and the development of individuals. His ideas about individual development support the thesis of SocioDynamic counselling that an individual should be assisted (by the counselling process) to move toward goals that he or she has reasons to value.

Sen argues that as competent human beings, we cannot shirk the task of judging the way things are, how they should be, and what we can do to change what needs changing. If help-seekers are to move toward goals in life that are valued, and thus expand personal freedom, counsellors need to keep the following questions in mind as the counselling dialogue unfolds:

1. What are the actual capabilities of this person—what does he or she *know how* to do?
2. What are the *potential* capabilities of this person—what might he or she be able to do if given an opportunity to learn or develop the capacity in question?
3. Do existing *social arrangements* support the person to use or learn to use capacities? If the answer is "no," then we have identified a block or barrier to the development of the individual's capacity, hence a restriction on the individual's personal freedom. Personal freedom depends upon the ability to choose; the ability to choose is tied directly to capacity. For example, an individual's capacity to choose is severely restricted if the individual does not have the capacity to read, to walk, or to think abstractly, and so on. When a person's capacity development is blocked, we have a case of unfreedom. When a person's capacity development is supported, there is the possibility of expanding the person's range of choices, hence expanding personal freedom.

We can regard the various things that a person may value doing or being as capacities. Capacities can be elementary, such as the ability to read or speak. They also can be more complex activities, such as the ability to secure adequate food and shelter, participate in community life, or carry out complex work. Personal states, such as achieving self-esteem or having a self-identity that is stable and fulfilling, are considered psychological capacities.

Capacity (including real opportunity for choice) is a kind of substantive freedom to achieve various lifestyles. It is extremely important to realize the vital role that choice plays in determining whether or not one can be said to have freedom. For example, a wealthy person may choose to fast and, thereby, have a very limited eating function. In fact, it may be the same as that of a destitute person who cannot afford to buy food. However, the wealthy person can choose whether or not to eat, while the destitute person cannot. Fasting is not the same thing as starving.

It is a fundamental purpose of SocioDynamic counselling to assist individuals in capacity building and achieving status in social relationships that support individual capacity development. In other words, one of the guiding principles of SocioDynamic counselling is that it is *good to expand individual capacity, choice, and freedom, and minimize or reduce unfreedoms.*[26]

One further distinction to make about choice and capacity involves the difference between *processes* that support freedom of decisions and actions and *opportunities* that individuals actually have, given their personal and social circumstances. Unfreedoms can stem either from failed processes, such as violation of civil rights, or from lack of real opportunity, such as conditions of forced starvation, absence of employment, or lack of educational facilities.

From the SocioDynamic perspective, counsellors should help individuals with capacity development in order to expand the range of choices open to an individual and to facilitate the reduction of unfreedoms that a person faces. Counsellors themselves should *value* the idea of personal freedom—that is, the capacity of the individual to choose goals and to develop capacity for moving toward goals she has reasons to value. This assertion is based on the premise that greater freedom (capacity and choice) improves the ability of people to help themselves and also influences the quality of social support arrangements.

Counsellors have many tools to use in assisting individuals to expand capacity and choice. Learning activities, life-space co-investigation and mapping, network development, dialogical communication, personal activity projects, development of "escape routes" from unfreedoms, conversion of information into personal knowledge, alteration of perspectives, and self-identity validation are some of the choice- and capacity-building activities that can be part of good counselling.

SocioDynamic Counselling Is a Wisdom-Based Practice

For many decades, an emphasis in counselling has been on the *effectiveness of counselling outcomes*. Of course, all counselling methods must be concerned that their application to the lives of individuals who are experiencing trouble is ameliorative. There should be no question about this. However, an equally, or even more important consideration is: Is this method of counselling promoting wise choices? Does it take advantage of the wisdom that is part of the cultural heritage of the help-seeker? Does this type of counselling help answer the question, "How *should* I live my life?" Is there a place for discussion of "spiritual" issues and spiritual choices with which a help-seeker is struggling? Does this type of counselling provide mental and emotional shelter and safety for the individual who is coping with difficult problems in his or her everyday life? Are the counsellor and the help-seeker able to generate good ideas about what to do and how to proceed, drawing from the stock of knowledge that counsellor and the help-seeker have as a result of being members of particular cultures?

Wisdom is not singular and thus cannot be defined in a final and precise manner. Wisdom is an array of better-than-ordinary ideas about how to live and how to solve problems of life. Further, different people in varying circumstances express wisdom differently. Minimally, wisdom involves

- *Reality seeking*, trying to see and perceive things as they are—letting others and things "speak to us" from their own constitution;
- *Identifying faulty assumptions* and resisting prejudicial and discriminatory ideas;
- *Acting in prudent and fruitful ways;*
- Acting from the *perspective of the whole;*
- Better-than-ordinary *grasp of the existential situation;*
- Knowledge of *when to act* and when not to act;
- Facing the world and problems with *peace of mind and compassion;*
- Having a *reflective and "critical thinking" attitude* toward ideas and problems in life;

- Developing a repertoire of *"good ideas"* that have stood the test of time and that are useful guides in how one ought to live in a particular cultural context;
- Being able to *anticipate problems* (based on life experience and study) and being able to avoid and/or deal with them in a mindful and effective manner;
- *Openness to lived experience* as a first-order reality; and
- *Appreciation for both contemplative and active stances in life.*

Abraham Maslow[27] studied self-actualizing (wise) people. In general, he found them to be more detached than non self-actualizers from the ordinary dictates of their culture. They did not consider themselves to be objects and did not subscribe uncritically to consumer culture. Central to their lives were what Maslow called *B-values*: wholeness, perfection, completion, justice, aliveness, richness, simplicity, beauty, goodness, uniqueness, effortlessness, playfulness, truth, honest, reality, and self-sufficiency. Wisdom implies mindfulness, an ethical outlook, creativity, and conscious awareness. These are excellent qualities for helpers to possess.

What does it mean to define counselling as a wisdom-based practice? In general, it means placing greater emphasis on "good" ideas and their evaluation and application to the question: How should I live my life? Further, the conception of wisdom-based counselling is compatible with a stance that helping is a practice governed by ethical decisions.

Wisdom-based helping acknowledges the value of placing trust in cultural sensibility and the know-how that comes from reflected-on life experience. Wisdom does not deny the value of technical, abstract theory and expert advice. It regards theoretical and technical expertise as important forms of knowledge along with other forms. Helping can be guided by both theory and cultural sensibility. *One should not preclude or exclude the other.* Still, quite often what help-seekers find useful is not theoretical explanations of their problems, but concrete examples of how other people have solved problems similar to those that they are confronting.

27

Many influences in contemporary society encourage a technological attitude and the commodification of humans and their social life activities. While technology and commodification serve market forces and corporate goals, they often undermine the human quality of individual existence. However, counsellors can assist help-seekers in attempts to "claw back" their personal existences toward a renewed respect for the human qualities of uniqueness, solidarity with others, and agency, if those are goals that they value. This means that SocioDynamic counselling tries to address *lifestyle* choice and *quality of life* issues, when appropriate to the help-seeker's need. This willingness to be interested in the individual's quality of life illustrates the holistic nature of SocioDynamic counselling.

This task of standing up for the "human factor" in daily life is important to members of the helping professions. It is the helping professions that purport to assist people to design, construct, and implement solutions to problems in everyday life. A wisdom-based helping practice can assist in the process of reaffirming the integrity of the individual as an agent and as a social actor effectively engaged in dialogical relations with others (Touraine).[28]

We also need to expand the horizons of counselling and acknowledge the importance of "spirituality" and the need to articulate and discuss spiritual concerns—a need that great numbers of people have—that are often considered "outside" the domain of counselling. Wisdom-based counselling practice validates the discussion of spiritual issues in the counselling process whenever spirituality is part of the help-seeker's concern and reason for seeking personal help.

The idea of spirituality should be flexible and expansive to include not only a wide range of traditional religious concerns, but also discussions of personal philosophy and inspiring ideas from literature and life and discussions about humanity's ecological connection with nature, all life, and the planet. In the full range of spirituality, the counsellor's role is not that of proselytizer, but that of partner-in-dialogue.

Elements of wisdom-based counselling
Elements of wisdom that seem to be critical in guiding the helping process and the helper are

- *A reality-seeking attitude.* What is actually going on here? How can the person be assisted to describe her experience and her interpretation of the existential situation, as she perceives it? By definition, reality seekers are open-minded, receptive, and flexible. They are careful not to settle into habitual ways of thinking, perceiving, and self-expression. They know that all explanations, theories, and models are at best crude and approximate maps of reality. They shun the "one right way" and either/or modes of thinking. Wise people are attentive. They do not shut out new ideas and cling to old conceptions that no longer fit emerging contexts. Reality seekers rely heavily on description and are cautious about theory and final explanations.
- *Acquiring a perspective of non-reactive acceptance.* The human is equipped with a *limbic* system and an intense array of emotions that accompany it—anger, disgust, revenge, jealousy, greed, craving, hatred, fear, and more. Through self-observation, wise persons have learned to recognize such reactions and take steps to prevent them from becoming long-standing states of mind. Further, they have learned how to prevent these emotional states from becoming translated into harmful action. Of course, wise people are not passive. They have learned how to guide their actions from reflection and not just from the limbic system. They are guided by intelligent thinking, compassion, patience, timing, awareness of self and others, goodness, and ethical values. They move toward peace, both individual and collective, rather than toward violent reaction and dominance in interaction.
- *Holistic perception.* A system, such as an individual, a family, a life-space, an institution, or culture, is a whole that consists of interactive, interdependent parts and persistent patterns of relationship. Too often we fix our attention on a part and lose sight of the patterns of influence that interact

with that part. This is why we should try not to separate different aspects of the person in the counselling process. Feelings, perceptions, actions, embodiment, and meaning all are interactive parts of the system we call a "person." Further, the person is bound up in relationships with the elements of his or her life-space.

- *An understanding of the "oneness" of human life* with all other forms of life and with the natural universe. This is the ecological wisdom that many aboriginal peoples have long had, but that has become lost to modern societies. As David Abram[29] has pointed out, from an ecologically wise point of view, it is not the statements that we make with our language tools that are "true" or "false," but the kind of relations we build and sustain with the rest of nature. An individual, or a community of people living in harmony and mutually beneficial relations with the surrounding natural world, can be described as "living in truth." This kind of truth we can only learn through the giving and receiving of stories—both autobiographical and cultural.
- *Actions that benefit others.* Wisdom-based helping practices can occur when helpers are able to use ethical principles and act on them with a resolve and frame of mind that unify intelligence, emotion, and imagination. One can act compassionately, for the benefit of and with respect for others, and with respect for oneself and one's own actions under the influence of this frame of mind.

Contemporary commercialized life is often in conflict with compassion, shared respect, and ethical reasoning. People everywhere speak of being overstressed, not having enough time, and finding no relief from the helter-skelter life of survival in a market economy. The stressed, hectic pace and manner of daily living in contemporary societies are a kind of assault against self-dignity, compassion, and inner peace. Everything is uncertain and risky, and there are few places to find shelter from the stresses of instrumental reasoning.

30

A wisdom-based helping practice tries to open possibilities for understanding the importance of quiet, patient, contemplative moments in life. It also works toward a restoration of a holistic view of people and their worlds, as well as of the larger world-planet. It tries to move individuals toward inclusion rather than exclusion, toward unity, both inward and outward, rather than separation. It strongly resists the conversion of humans into objects and commodities. At the same time, it tries to help people build perspectives and paths in life that allow them to experience success in their social worlds.

Wisdom-based counselling supports the principle of personal freedom constituted from choice and capability. It recognizes the social nature of human existence and society. Hence, it underwrites the need to be responsible, both personally and socially. Wisdom-based counselling is concerned with being good (Blackburn),[30] as well as doing good. To act in helpful ways toward others is an ethical "good" in all known cultures, independent of doctrine and ideology.

I would like now to add the voices of four philosophers to this discussion of the SocioDynamic philosophy of helping: the Danish philosophers, Søren Kierkegaard (1813-1855) and Knud Løgstrup (1905-1981); the Russian literary theorist, Mikhail Bakhtin (1895-1975); and the German philosopher of existence, Karl Jaspers (1883-1969). I believe that each embodies ideas of significance for SocioDynamic counselling that deepen the discussion of the SocioDynamic philosophy of helping.

The ideas on ethical conduct put forward by Søren Kierkegaard and Knud Løgstrup are highly informing for helpers. Although they lived in different eras and did not share the same way of thinking, both wrote philosophical insights of importance for contemporary helpers.

The existential voice of Søren Kierkegaard
In an earlier book, I distilled certain ideas from Kierkegaard, which many readers found inspiring. I am including this material as a fictive lecture, slightly altered from his own words written in his book, *The Point of View of My Work as an Author.* If Kierkegaard

31

were alive today and we invited him to give us a brief "lecture" on the essence of helping, I believe he would speak to us in the following words:

One must first take the pains to find the other where the other is and begin there. This is the secret of the art of helping others. *Anyone who does not master this is himself deluded when he proposes to help others. In order to help another, I must first understand more than she—yet first of all I must surely understand what she understands. If I do not know that, then my greater understanding will be of no help to her.*

If, however, I am disposed to plume myself on my greater understanding, I am vain or proud. At the bottom, instead of benefiting her, I want to be admired. But all true helping begins with self-humbling; the helper must first humble himself and not set himself over and above the one he would help. To help another does not mean to dominate or act intrusively, but to serve. To help does not mean to be ambitious, but to be patient.

To help means to endure for the time being the imputation that one does not know and, at the outstart, does not understand what the other understands. Be the amazed listener who sits and hears what the other finds more delight in telling you because you listen in amazement. *For example, take the case of one who comes to you filled with passionate anger. Begin with the other as though it were the other who had to instruct you (in his reasons for anger), and do it in such a way that the angry person—who was too impatient to listen to a single word of yours—yet finds in you an attentive and receptive listener; if you cannot do that, you cannot help him at all.*

Kierkegaard created these ideas in 1848, but they were not published as a book until after his death in 1855. In this brief "lecture," he provides insightful ideas about what a helper must do to be truly helpful. What he presented as good ideas about helping is still valid today, especially the following:

1. Listen from the perspective of the other.
2. Listen with a fresh ear and allow yourself to be amazed at what you hear.

3. Exercise patience, respect, and equality.
4. Begin where the other is, not where you expect, assume, or need them to be.
5. Come to the helping situation in a state of not-knowing; let the other teach you.
6. Restrain your own vanity, self-importance, and need to assert yourself.

These observations are valuable contributions to the philosophy of helping that informs the practice of SocioDynamic counselling.

The ethical voice of Knud Løgstrup

Knud Ejler Løgstrup (1905-1981) was born in Copenhagen and is considered by many to be the most influential Danish moral philosopher of this century. He disagreed strongly with the Christian tenets of Kierkegaard's existentialism. For Løgstrup there was no "Christian" morality, nor any secular morality. He believed that there is only human morality. He offered a different understanding of interpersonal life, based on natural trust. For him, distrust is learned; trust is natural and is given by virtue of being born a human.

I have distilled some of Løgstrup's insights in a way that shows the importance of his thought for counsellors and the profession of helping. I have slightly altered some of his sentences, but have done so in a way that does not change his meaning, as I understand it. Most of the ideas that follow are taken from his book, *The Ethical Demand.*[31]

Although we make our "self," we do not make our life—that is given to us at birth. A basic, natural feature of human life is trust. Without trust, life would not be possible. This condition of trust *places an ethical demand on us with regard to others. That demand is that we must recognize, respect, and care for that part of another's life that he or she places before us in genuine conversation. It is natural in human life to treat each other with trust, whether the encounter is with one who is familiar or is a stranger. Only because of some special circumstance do we regard others with distrust.*

To trust is to lay one's self open. That is why we react so strongly when our trust is betrayed. A breach of trust is very serious. When one has approached the other in an open, accepting manner and trust is abused, the emotions that are brought forth are strong and often make resolution and subsequent trust impossible or, at the very least, extremely difficult to establish.

In a condition of distrust, communication becomes black and white, accusations and suspicion abound. Trust, in contrast, is a kind of self-surrender. When that opening of self is rejected, the result is moral accusations. The self-opening must be covered over. In its basic sense, trust is essential to every genuine conversation (dialogue) if understanding is to occur.

The essence of interpersonal communication and the ethical demand made by coexistence arises from just this: one person daring to lay himself or herself open to another in the hope of a trustful and validating response. Trust and distrust are not two parallel ways of being.

Distrust is deficient trust. The demand for trust is a characteristic of human life, it is not something that a person can decide to give or not. The demand is always there because it is part of the life that we were given at birth. However, the individual does decide, in each human encounter, what the content of that trust will be. The demand to take care of another person's life is always there. How that care is to be given, in what ways, and how much is decided by the individual in each encounter. It is up to the individual to use whatever intelligence, imagination, and resourcefulness he or she has to determine what the ethical demand requires and how to respond to it.

Basic trust and communication can be perverted in various ways. One way is to resort to "polite" communication in which important things are not said or heard because they are judged impolite. In polite conversation, much that is said is determined by the belief that "This is what the other expects or wants to hear" or by the rule that says, "This is what one should say in order to be polite."

A second perversion of trust and communication is the belief that we can only trust, and speak trustfully, to those who are

34

familiar to us. In fact, the opposite is often more nearly the case. Through familiarity, persons often learn how to avoid topics that should be discussed, but which they do not discuss for fear of disturbing the easiness or laziness of familiarity.

A third form of perversion of trust and communication is thinking that we know better than others do and wanting to change them. Having a belief that one knows what is the case better than others do, knowing what "ought to be done," often indicates a closed-mindedness in which understanding and trust are suspended. In a state of "knowing better," trust is often demanded or ignored; arrogance and imposition prevail and are likely to replace trust.

The ethical claim that life makes on us as beings endowed naturally with trust has a dual relationship to certainty. If I take on the norms and standards of social life as mine and consider trustworthiness primarily from the perspective of these norms, then I can rule out negotiation with the other and judgement that is shaped by dialogue, and can use these "norms" to lord it over the other. This turns the matter of taking care of a part of the other person's life into an uncertainty. Adherence to norms may take precedence over acting in trust and considering that exceptions must be allowed in some circumstances.

However, if by "certain" we mean that the situation under consideration—including that part of the other's life that is in question and the factors that impinge upon it—is clear, or as clear as it can be made, then this type of "certainty" does not dissolve into uncertainty.

I interpret Løgstrup's message along the following lines: As helpers, our will to do what is good for the other person, to speak or remain silent, or to act in harmony with our belief about what is best for another must always be joined with a willingness to let the other remain sovereign in his or her own world. The demand that we care for that part of the other person's life that has been opened to us, regardless of what the demand may indicate, is also a demand that the other be given time and opportunity to make his or her world as expansive as possible. Our care and trust should come in such as way as to free the other person from unreasonable constraint and give his or her vision the widest possible horizon.

The dialogical voice of Mikhail Bakhtin

The third philosophical voice I want to bring to bear on the ethical aspects of SocioDynamic counselling is that of the Russian literary theorist, Mikhail Bakhtin (1895-1975). He is famous for his insights into the dialogical nature of human existence—especially for contrasting dialogical voice with authoritative voice. Dialogical voice is reciprocal and co-constructive; in contrast, authoritative voice is monological and impositional. Bakhtin cautioned that we should oppose turning people into objects and that we should realize that human beings are constantly evolving. We cannot finalize or "completely know" another as long as that other lives. No finality of the other occurs until she has uttered her final words. If Bakhtin were alive today and giving a lecture, we would probably hear approximately the following passage from his 1984 book *Problems of Dostoevsky's Poetics*:

The truth about a person (as contained in the words of others), not directed to the person dialogically and therefore a second-hand truth, becomes a lie, degrading and deadening him. The consciousness of other people cannot be perceived, analyzed, defined as objects or as things—one can only truly relate to others dialogically. To think about others means to talk with them. Otherwise others immediately turn to us their objectified side. They fall silent, close up, and congeal into finished objectified images. Truth is not born nor is it to be found inside the head of an individual person, it is born between people who are collectively searching for truth in the process of their dialogic interaction.[32]

Bakhtin once remarked that it helps to think of a self as being a hotel with many rooms. In each of these rooms a voice has taken up residence. For example, when a person has never cooked or has had little or no experience in cooking, there is no "voice of the cook" in that self. However, after several years of experience of cooking, and perhaps taking some courses in cooking, reading about cooking, and cooking many different foods, then one has a voice of a cook. A room that is part of the hotel that that person is now has a resident voice—that of a "cook."

This example points out what Bakhtin and now others refer to as polyphony, or multi-vocality. Once a voice has taken up residence in the hotel of the self, it never completely goes away. It may become very much in the background, but it can always be called forth to speak again as the voice (of experience) that it is.

Fifty years as a practical counsellor and psychologist have taught me that it is almost always better to come to the counselling conversation with an attitude of trust and work hard to maintain conditions of trust. Trust (and the condition of respect that accompanies trust) is constitutive of good counselling. Of course, I know that often the other will not bring the same attitude of trust, but that attitude frequently changes as we proceed in a conversation in which I take a trusting part and in which I patiently try to understand the other's reasons for distrust and extend respect to the other.

My experience has also taught me that when I take the position of the "amazed listener," as advocated by Kierkegaard, and extend trust, then an openness occurs in which the other does lay out some part of his or her life experience for our mutual consideration.

Further, it is up to me to acknowledge the ethical claim that I protect and care for that part of life that comes to me. Just how I am able to do that and what it is that I do, are dependent upon many aspects of the particular helping situation. What I try hard not to do is shirk my responsibility to care and to act helpfully within the limits of my capacity, time, and opportunity.

Frequently, trust and responsive dialogue result in the help-seeker becoming oriented more toward self-helpfulness and saying in effect, "I have participated in a valuable and self-affirming conversation," or even better, "I did this myself."

Help-seekers who are discouraged, angry, silent, or demanding do not eliminate the factor of trust and care; they just make its attainment more difficult. Similarly, helpers who assume the personas of objectivity, expertise, arrogance, or officiousness do not eliminate the possibility of trust; they just make it much less probable.

To every extent possible, helpers should stand on the side of the other seeking help and see them as fellow members of a common humanity. Efforts to objectify and tendencies to label and classify others should be constrained. The kind of objectivity that counts in counselling is the "objectivity"—to the degree that this is possible—that a helper turns inwardly as a form of self-observation. This enables the helper to identify better and restrain prejudiced ideas and dismissive emotional reactions toward help-seekers who are different or difficult. To reiterate, as much as possible, it is desirable to remain attentively subjective and open to the other's meanings and life experience, as he or she describes and articulates these, and to remain self-observing and "objective" toward one's own reactions.

Karl Jaspers: Each person is a process of self-creation

I will finish my remarks on SocioDynamic counselling as a wisdom-based practice with a distillation of certain ideas that Karl Jaspers presented in his 1957 book, *Man in the Modern Age*.[33] The late professor Jaspers (1883-1969) was a German existential philosopher and psychiatrist. He is known as the originator of the "philosophy of existenz." The following are his words, slightly revised, and presented as an imaginary lecture:

We live in a time of techno-mass order in which persons must find and create "guidance from the inside" if they are to have successful lives—in other words, if the individual is to take a decisive grip upon the mechanism of his or her life and establish self-dependence as an independent individual.

All the while, one must form ties with others on a solid base of trust. If one is to get a firm grip on one's own life and form ties with others on the basis of trust, then a philosophy to live by is essential. Only by judging which ideas are good to live by and which are not, can the individual create himself or herself as an independent being secure in the experience of trustworthy relationships.

In the midst of rapidly changing and fluid, swarming societies we must remember that each human is more than he or she knows of himself or herself. Each person is not just one thing, once and for all, but is a process of self-creation. Each can make something of himself or herself by the activities of life that he or she can undertake, and that he or she decides on and does undertake. A sense of self-identity is the supreme instrument of knowledge. *Yet it supplies insight and vision only so long as it 1) remains aware of itself, 2) remains cognizant of the surrounding world, 3) is active in creating a life that has meaning, and 4) is tied to others by relationships of respect and trust.*

In presenting features of the philosophy of helping that serve as a foundation for SocioDynamic helping, I have been describing what is often referred to as the many elements of the counsellor's attitude. The counsellor's attitude is more important than all the specific counselling skills and techniques together. Who you are as a person, how you perceive and interpret the world of which you are a part, how you perceive and respond to other people, and the perceptions you hold toward yourself—these perceptions and interpretations guide your actions in the existential world of your experience.

The profound importance of counsellor attitude gives meaning to the maxim: You are your own method. In this time of techno-global mass societies, a wise counsellor encourages others to participate in self-created and co-created identity- and capacity-building projects, from their own resources. Helpers also will do well to remember that building self-esteem and dignity can best be done through trustworthy social ties with others. These conditions apply to all aspects of a person's life-space: home, work, learning, play, health, and spirituality.

Joint Action, Not Singular Action

The *joint action* of helper and help-seeker—listening together, thinking together, feeling together, and constructing together—will contribute to good counselling. The value of counselling results from coordinating and assembling the *joint* knowledge, intelligence, creativity, and wisdom of helper and help-seeker into a useful response to such questions as: "What is going on in my situation of concern? What should I perceive, learn, know, and do in order to move forward in my life? What are my next steps? How should I live my life?"

However, the SocioDynamic perspective acknowledges that a person is simultaneously a social actor, engaging in interaction and dialogue as a social partner, and a moral agent, making decisions and acting as a self-responsible individual. Without our sociality, we could not have selves and society. Without agency, we could not create distinctive biographies and history.

Showing Respect Is a Social Good

A core value in SocioDynamic helping is *respect:* for the uniqueness and integrity of persons who seek help, for the relationship and process of counselling, and for self. One of the principal means of showing respect is to validate the personal meanings and experiences of help-seekers. Self-validation and having one's own personal experience validated are needs common to people everywhere. Experience is the soil from which the seeds of insight, meaning, and action can grow. The counselling process cultivates the seeds that grow in the soil of experience.

Perspectives Guide Actions

What we perceive, think, imagine, and feel—our perspective and the configurations of meaning that form our conscious awareness at any moment in time—provide the guiding context for shaping our actions. Therefore, it is essential to gain entry into the life-space of the other so that the reasons for the other's perceptions and actions can become knowledge for our use in understanding him or her. Toward any given object of attention, there will always be differing perceptions/perspectives by different individuals on its nature and meaning. For example, imagine that five people are sitting in a room when a bear walks in the door. Depending upon the streams of experience that make up the life history of each individual, there is almost certain to be a range of perspectives toward the bear, leading to a range of reactions:

Perspective	Action
• The bear is dangerous	and must be killed.
• The bear is hungry	and must be avoided.
• The bear is at risk	and must be protected.

40

- The bear is friendly   and therefore I will approach it.
- The bear is fascinating   and I would like to observe it.

Self-Creation (Homo Creator)—An Empowering Image to Guide and Inspire the Practice of Counselling

A basic premise of the SocioDynamic perspective is that nearly all help-seekers are creative and active persons with potential capacities for constructing solutions and answers to their own dilemmas. They also possess the capacity to guide their own lives, given the proper learning environment and freedom from interference from both internal and external influence and constraint.

Readiness—Not Resistance—A Preferred Concept for Understanding Why Help-Seekers Do or Do Not Participate Willingly in Counselling Dialogue

All experienced counsellors know that help-seekers often seem passive and disempowered. They may be angry or demanding of the counsellor and actively reject what the counsellor tries to offer. However, even persons who act in these difficult ways are still potentially capable of creative action. Help-seekers who come to counselling in demanding or passive modes usually have experienced frustration, deprivation, and interference in their lives to a point where they cannot cope adequately. When one is blocked or overwhelmed by circumstances in life, it is not easy to be a tranquil person.

When faced with anger and defiance, counsellors should realize that they are not the legitimate targets of help-seeker negativity. Further, they should be able to curb their own tendencies to react defensively. In this way, they are in a position to keep a more balanced view of the negativity of others and to find ways to begin building common ground.

The helper should regard individuals who demonstrate negativity or passivity as *not ready* for participating in constructive problem solving. Then the first task for the counsellor is to create conditions that promote readiness on the part of the help-seeker to communicate, learn, and engage in forward movement *before* moving on to problem solving. Many times counselling will fail because the counsellor is unaware of the need to build a constructive basis for cooperation before moving to a search for solutions. A conversation that is sensible to both help-seeker and helper must come first. Then some degree of dialogue can occur, and at least a small island of common ground can be found or created. Little headway will be made in resolving concerns brought to counselling unless common ground and a sensible conversation are established first.

The Counselling Process Provides an Enhanced Learning Environment

The challenge for the helper is how to use ideas and practices that create an enhanced learning environment within which the process of self-creation can proceed. It is not the task of the helper to diagnose and cure faults in the personality of the help-seeker, nor is it the task of the helper to "fix" the other's concern. SocioDynamic counselling is not a prescriptive process and tries to avoid all postures that patronize or condescend.

SocioDynamic helping is driven by a participatory, constructive, self-creative impulse, and not by an advising, adjusting, fixing impulse. Counsellors and help-seekers function best when an interactive, cooperative, open-minded, and negotiating relationship is established with each other. These are the relational features that enable the creativity and intelligence of helper and help-seeker to function jointly and improve the chances for generating forward movement in the life of the help-seeker.

Position of "Both Knowing"

In conventional counselling models, it is often assumed that only the counsellor "knows best," and therefore, the counsellor can, and should, give advice and prescribe solutions for the problems of others.

In SocioDynamic Counselling, *both* helper and help-seeker are active knowers, and each may "know best," but about different things. The counsellor is an expert on providing optimal learning conditions and on skilful interpersonal communication. The help-seeker is an expert on his or her own life experience.

42

No one, neither the counsellor nor anyone else, ever will be as familiar with the life experience of a help-seeker as the help-seeker herself. A help-seeker also "knows best" about the goals she values in life. Of course the help-seeker may not be able to articulate her life experience in lucid ways and may have little previous experience in expressing her life experience. Having knowledge of one's experience and being able to articulate that knowledge are two different processes. Another way of saying this is that a person often "knows more than he or she can say."

This is where the counsellor's ability to use skilful interpersonal communication and capacity to communicate what is experienced comes into play. The SocioDynamic counselling process does not contain one expert and one dummy. Instead, it includes two individuals, each of whom has important contributions to make to the counselling process. Good counselling results from joint efforts at problem solving and not from expert advice.

Advice Giving Can Go Wrong

It is well to remember that there are at least three reasons to be wary of advice giving. First, any advice given may be the wrong advice. Second, it may be good advice, but applied wrongly by the advice receiver. Third, if the advice, be it good or bad, does not produce desirable results, then the stage is set for the advice receiver to blame the advice giver for having given poor advice. This means that advice giving runs the danger of encouraging the avoidance of responsibility on the part of the help-seeker. It is essential to distinguish between advice and information. Advice giving is at best a risky business. However, providing accurate information at appropriate times and in meaningful ways is essential.

A SocioDynamic Credo for Counselling

~

Fellow human beings, we are in this world together. Let us find ways to combine our intelligence, creativity, and experience on behalf of goals that you value. If we work together, we may be able to create better conditions for you and your life than either of us alone can achieve. The very act of joining together in a common effort to find a better path for you will make my life better also.

~

SocioDynamic counselling is a way of thinking about people, what they are trying to create in life, and what either impedes or supports their efforts. How can counsellors engage constructively in assisting individuals to move toward those goals in life that they value and choose?

~

Everyday living is a dynamic process—a conversation. Cultures, societies, and civilizations are conversations. Families, workgroups, and relationships are conversations. Dialogical conversations are the best methods that people have invented for negotiating with each other, the best methods they have for thinking together and building together and for showing respect to each other. Counselling, at its best, is dialogue in the service of human need.

~

Career is from the Latin *carrus*, meaning passage, course, or wheeled chariot. One's career is one's life. In this sense, all counselling is career counselling, since all counselling is about one's life. Counselling itself is a course through life. This is so because we, as counsellors, are constantly changing, evolving—today we are different from what we were yesterday. We, and those we help, are fellow human beings—this we must not forget.

All counselling is also personal—counselling is a process between two or more persons. Persons are persons *and* personal, they are not products, objects, labels, classifications, or categories. To confuse persons and objects is to make a profound categorical mistake. Thus we can say that counselling is a personal (interpersonal) method of life planning.

~

When Is Counselling Good?

Counselling is good when help-seekers feel no imposition,
When the counsellor brings clarity and compassion,
Not so good when help-seekers are told what to do,
Worst when they feel betrayed or violated.

Fail to respect others, and they fail to respect you.
But of a good counsellor, who talks little, but
Listens carefully and understands much,
When the work of counselling is done,
And the purpose of counselling fulfilled,
Help-seekers will say: "We did this ourselves."
Such good counselling is possible when
The counsellor knows that she can only bring forth that
Which already lies half-dawning in the help-seeker's own mind.

(Inspired by ideas from Lao-Tzu's *The Way* and
the poems of K. Gibran)

Chapter 3: SocioDynamic
Counselling Practice

This chapter describes practical ideas and activities that constitute the vocabulary and practice of SocioDynamic counselling. Since the philosophy and the practice of SocioDynamic counselling are closely interwoven, the reader will find some repetition of ideas that were presented in the preceding chapters.

My presentation in this chapter is based on the assumption that readers will already have some knowledge and experience with counselling or another helping profession, such as psychology or social work. Many of these ideas also have significance for other professions, such as nursing, teaching, consulting, and managing.

Moves in the Game of Counselling

As mentioned earlier, I think of counselling as a type of language game. I like the metaphor of "counselling-as-game" because it implies: 1) "players" (counsellors and help-seekers); 2) "moves" (functions and tactics—for example, listening or mapping—are moves); and 3) tools (what counsellors use to accomplish moves—for example, metaphor is used to change levels of meaning, or computers are used to access information). Moves and tools are often closely related or even identical. For example, questioning is a move, the question is a tool. Often a move can be made using a variety of tools. For example, if your move is to *include the other*, possible tools for accomplishing this move are sentences that invite, shared humour, joining the other in an activity, putting an arm around the other's shoulder, conveying appreciation for the other or their actions, asking the other for help, or sitting closer rather than farther away. Each of these tools can also be construed as a "move."

I also like the analogy of a game, partly because in a game it is very important not just to see what the other is doing, but also to foresee what his, and my, next moves might be. As a matter of perception, I must be firmly rooted in the immediate present of our dialogue. Yet I must at the same time keep an imaginative foreseeing openness to what is only emerging as a probable future. When playing a game of ball, for example, a good player does not throw the ball to where the other player is at this instant but to where he foresees the player to be at the time the ball arrives. Games, including the game of counselling, are played according to rules, but there is inevitably a degree of indeterminacy about what move each player will make next. What I am describing as foreseeing is also called "peripheral vision" by Mary Catherine Bateson,[34] an unusually perceptive cultural anthropologist who sees more nuances of a situation and a wider horizon of the context than does the ordinary perceiver. Human understanding is neither pre-given nor final; it is emergent.

An Essential Caveat

My use of game as a metaphor for counselling requires one essential caveat. Unlike most games, the object of the game of counselling is *not* to win. The goal is to co-produce, on behalf of the help-seeker, results, such as clarified understanding, insight, articulation of experience, critical reasoning, initiatives to develop capacity, solutions, self-esteem, plans, fulfillment of needs, relief from suffering, social support, and increased capacity to participate in social life activities.

A fundamental rule for the game of counselling is that it is a *cooperative activity*, rather than a competitive activity. While maintaining appropriate boundaries for a counselling relationship, the greater the attunement of each player to the other, the higher the probability of achieving successful results.

Counselling practice has a logic, but it is not the logic of the logician. It is a "fuzzy" logic that perceives and constantly adjusts to evolving realities. At the same time, it has a logic of coherence. In counselling there is always an effort to get things to hang together, to cohere—we wish to get the whole picture, hear the complete story. Yet at the same time, we know that there are constantly changing details in an individual's life-space, each of which can assume considerable importance, or not.

To play the game of counselling, one must become good at using words and other language tools, for language tools are our means of "making moves." As I prepared to write this chapter, I consulted *Webster's Third New International Dictionary* to find out what meanings were given to the word *move*. The great range of meanings that define *move* surprised me. Some of the meanings that are relevant to use of *move* (or *moves*) in the game of counselling are:

> To go forward, to get more fully worked out through successive details, to leave one place and go to a new one, to exhibit outward activity, to comport oneself in a specified way, to rouse to doing something by reason of being a motive or incentive or influence, a step taken so as to gain some objective, to cause or arouse into an emotional state of feeling, to actuate.

Tools for Getting Things Done in Counselling

According to the Russian psychologist Lev Vygotsky,[35] people use three types of tools to get things done in human interaction: 1) psychological (symbolic) tools, 2) technical tools, and 3) mediators (self-as-tool). I choose to call symbolic-linguistic tools by the name *mental* tools. From the SocioDynamic perspective, all humanly invented tools are referred to as *cultural tools* and are composed of two types of tools: technical and mental.

A *technical tool* refers to a non-symbolic object, such as a computer, chair, engine, pencil, cup, radio, and so on. Many technical tools are complex and are made of technical components integrated into a single larger tool. All technical tools are human inventions and, therefore, are cultural artifacts.

A *mental* tool (in Vygotsky's terms, a "psychological" tool) is symbolic. Hence, all language phenomena—single sounds, the alphabet, words, and sentences, and very complex mental tools, such as stories, texts, diagrams, maps, musical scores, dramas, and works of literature—are mental tools. These are also human inventions and, therefore, can also be considered to be cultural artifacts.

It may seem obvious, but I have discovered that most people, including many counsellors, have not realized the importance of construing words as tools. Humans use words to get things done. For example, the simple sentence, "Please stand up," is a tool for getting a person to stand up. In their daily work, counsellors often use both technical and mental tools.

Technical tools, such as computers, telephones, pencils, paper, chairs, and tape recorders, are essential to the work of the contemporary counsellor. Counsellors use an even greater range of mental tools—words, sentences, ideas, metaphors, stories, intonation, texts, pictures, diagrams, maps, models—to do counselling. The significance attributed to the term *tools* in the SocioDynamic vocabulary is based on the following ideas:

- All tools (both mental and technical) are human inventions.
- Humans use mental tools to describe and redescribe selves, social interactions, human activity, and society.
- Tools are used by people to get things done—a tool implies a specific function or set of functions.

The concept *tool* is used to replace partially the concept *psychological technique*.

Moves and Tools Combine to Make Strategies

The value of any move or tool in the game of counselling is influenced by a variety of helper- and help-seeker-based factors, including competency, experience, stage of the game, needs of the players, meaningfulness of the participation, knowledge of possible moves, and individual perspectives. Tools and moves are learned. They imply functionality. The important question to ask of any tool or move is, "What does using this move/tool get done?"

In the rest of this chapter, I present basic helping strategies, each of which is composed of several tools and moves. While reading a chapter in a small book cannot make a counsellor of anyone, the purpose of this chapter is to give the reader a feel for the practice of SocioDynamic counselling.

A SocioDynamic counselling strategy is not composed of a defined number of steps or parts. Spontaneity and inventiveness are important SocioDynamic principles. A counsellor should always be prepared to invent and modify counselling strategies and use different tools and moves, depending upon the particulars of each counselling session. The strategies are meant to provide guidance and stimulate the creativity and inventiveness of the counselor but are not meant to be prescriptions or formulas.

This approach to using "suggestive strategies" that encourage improvisation and spontaneity, rather than prescriptive interventions that objectify behaviour, is based on two assumptions: 1) persons are self-creating; and 2) all forms of helping, including counselling, are culturally define An effort to be helpful that makes sense in one cultural context may be nonsense in another. Therefore, counsellors must adjust to the specific cultural contexts in which counselling takes place.

These twelve SocioDynamic counselling strategies will be discussed in detail:

1. General SocioDynamic counselling strategy,
2. Dialogical listening,
3. Mindful problem solving,
4. Intelligent conversation,
5. Visualization and life-space mapping,
6. Personal projects,
7. Guided participation,
8. Future-building,
9. Self-authoring,
10. Bricolage,
11. Empathic attunement, and
12. Group counselling and other social supports.

A General SocioDynamic Counselling Strategy

The SocioDynamic counselling strategy is based on four assumptions:

1. Social life presents a multiplicity of constraints and opportunities.
2. Individuals are both self-creating and co-created through interactions with others and with environmental conditions.

51

3. Most solutions are temporary, co-constructed, and optimal when based on the resources and capacities of the help-seeker.

Using ideas, reflected-on experience, data, and dialogue, people can construct and revise their perspectives as a basis for new and effective pathways of action.

Figure 1. General SocioDynamic Counselling Strategy: a creative-co-constructive process.

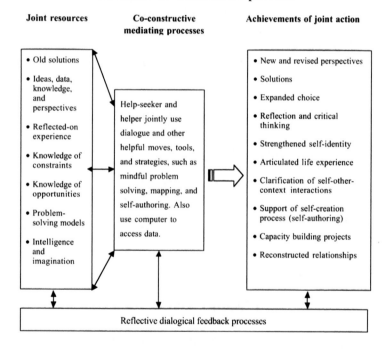

Joint resources	Co-constructive mediating processes	Achievements of joint action
• Old solutions • Ideas, data, knowledge, and perspectives • Reflected-on experience • Knowledge of constraints • Knowledge of opportunities • Problem-solving models • Intelligence and imagination	Help-seeker and helper jointly use dialogue and other helpful moves, tools, and strategies, such as mindful problem solving, mapping, and self-authoring. Also use computer to access data.	• New and revised perspectives • Solutions • Expanded choice • Reflection and critical thinking • Strengthened self-identity • Articulated life experience • Clarification of self-other-context interactions • Support of self-creation process (self-authoring) • Capacity building projects • Reconstructed relationships

Reflective dialogical feedback processes

This general counselling strategy (see Figure 1) is a suggested template to guide the counselling process. It should be modified to meet the demands of the particular help-seeker's problem and existential situation. It is based on the assumption that counselling is best when it joins the resources of both helper and help-seeker in a joint effort to construct and negotiate useful solutions that have personal meaning for the help-seeker.

Figure 2: Listening: The Helping Strategy
That Enables Other Strategies

The daily discipline of listening and responding to meaning is obedience. The concept of obedience is far more comprehensive than the narrow notion of doing-what-you-are-told-to-do. Obedience in the full sense is the process of attuning the heart to the simple call contained in the complexity of a given situation.

David Steindl-Rast[36]

Listening betrayed

But what I really dislike in myself is when I cannot hear the other person because I am so sure in advance of what he is about to say that I don't listen. It is only afterward that I realize that I have heard only what I have already decided he is saying. I have failed really to listen. Or even worse are those times when I can't hear because what he is saying is too threatening, and might even make me change my views or behaviour. Still worse are those times when I catch myself trying to twist his message to make it say what I want him to say, and then hearing only that.

Carl Rogers[37]

The single most powerful tool that a helper possesses is the ability to listen deeply, with concentration, and with an unbroken desire to understand the other's meanings. All methods of counselling use effective listening as the essential communication skill upon which the entire process of helping rests.

Various labels are applied to the kind of listening that is valued in counselling. The most widely used terms are *active listening* and *empathic listening*.[38] The form of communication advocated for SocioDynamic counselling is *dialogical communication;* therefore, listening is referred to as *dialogical listening.*

The process of dialogical listening ties together the internal state of the listener, the nature of the relations between listener and speaker, and the overall transformative learning process of which listening is a part and to which it contributes. I think of these aspects of listening as

- Inner peace,
- Harmonious relations, and
- Transformative learning.

Inner peace
One of the greatest obstacles to listening is a distracted or turbulent and conflicted state of mind on the part of the listener. Of course, it is not easy to achieve a quiet, inward state of mind. To do this means to put aside, at least for the moment, one's own ego urgings, agenda for what should be said and heard, and the fears and ideas one may have regarding lack of time, busy schedule, getting the job finished quickly—in short, all of the worries about failing to meet the time constraints imposed by self, others, and the working situation.

Zen writers sometimes write of the "monkey mind." By this, they are referring to the hectic and constantly changing attention of a distracted mind. It is like a monkey tied to a stake. It leaps this way and that, going at great bursts of speed, but not getting anywhere.

Martin Buber[39] has written about "making present." If we desire a genuine meeting with another, we do not face him or her in the abstract or behind a veil of secrecy but as a bodily presence. We make ourselves present to the other through the actions of our body, especially our "human face." To make oneself present to others means to come to a full stop before them, release one's attention from earlier events and future events as well, and remain quietly receptive to them for a continuing time. It also means putting your own needs in abeyance for the time being so that you are liberated to recognize and respond to the expressed needs of the other and also to your relationship with him or her.

What is it like to experience peace of mind? It is akin to being in a cathedral where every sound can register in your consciousness. The ring of the other's words is like the pure tones of a temple bell. You receive the other's words and tone of voice without expecting that he or she should say or be other than what you receive. Peace of mind is multi-dimensional. It is

- Receptive (takes in others' voices as rich sources of meaning),
- Still (a deep well of silence),
- Concentrated (ready with heart, mind, and spirit focussed on another),
- Respectful (hears me as I am, not as others expect or believe I am),
- Patient (there is a time and a place for everything under the sun),
- Empty of self (this space, in which I hear you, is *for you*; I stand aside and hold my ego needs in check),
- Aware of its own mood (every understanding has its own mood, and the mood in which I am immersed will colour what I am able to hear), and
- Appreciative (your words will teach me, and for that I am thankful).

Peace of mind is both a spiritual and a psychological achievement. Psychological processes and philosophical thinking can make contributions to peace of mind. Some of the more helpful psychological processes are the following:

55

- Reflect on experience, with an intention to sort out what is important and what is not, so far as the experience of the counselling process is concerned, and reflect on how one's frame of mind influences what he or she is able to hear.
- Sitting or walking quietly and letting one's mind ebb and flow with whatever is seeking a hearing, refraining from "trying" to think about any specific topic, are excellent pre-listening practices. *Try to "let go" and allow the flow of mind to present itself without conscious direction.* Later, it is a good idea to make notes of any thoughts, ideas, or possibilities that presented themselves during the letting-go period. Experiencing "letting go" of periods of conscious cognitive control and experiencing the free flow of one's own mind, are good preparations for listening. The human mind is a self-organizing system. To a degree, we must learn how not to interfere with its healthy, creative, self-organizing activity.
- Another way to clear one's mind of distractions is to *become silent and breathe quietly for a minute or two before changing to a new task or activity.* Don't try to think of anything, just settle and join in the flow of mind. Don't try to direct or channel your consciousness toward anything in particular. Let the remnants of your immediately preceding experience (such as the previous counselling session) fade from your mind. It is very important to begin each new task with a fresh mind and not allow the clutter of the past moments (or hours, days, or months) to interfere with the new situation you are entering into. Strive to face each successive task as if it were fresh, as though you were experiencing it for the first time.
- Learn to be *guided by a sense of personal time* and do not allow the self to become the slave of clock time. Or, if already the slave of clock and calendar, experiment with ways of recovering some of the personal freedom that comes with expanding one's personal control of the experience of time. Of course, when a counsellor works in an office or has some institutional role, there are clear expectations about the

amount of time a task should take. That is unfortunate, since the time expectation is seldom matched to the actual demands of the task, nor could it be in any absolute sense.

Yet even within the constraints of clock and calendar time, it is still possible to develop and pursue thinking and acting from the perspective of personal time—that is, time as it is actually experienced (not yet, now, no longer now, slow, fast, forgotten, dragging and going on forever, quick as a flash, timeless, etc.). To give oneself over to the clock and calendar is to open the door to constant and never-ending distractions, interruptions, and the experience of stress arising out of unmet expectations and lack of personal control.

The real secret of gaining a sense of personal time under one's own control is to reorganize activities in life so that excessive demands are reduced and a priority of importance for activities can be established. This leads to the possibility of being able to undertake each activity with a fresh mind capable of resisting distraction and interferences. In Zen, this is often called bringing the mind to a single point. It is this "mind at a single point" that makes deep and lucid listening possible.

More generally, in order to increase a capacity for good listening, it helps to work at living life consciously, especially in relation to the care extended toward body and mind. This means giving attention to adequate rest, healthy eating, exercising, resisting addictive substances, and providing one's mind with spiritual sustenance. This can range from such traditional practices as prayer, meditation, yoga, or study of inspirational writings, to communing with nature, participating in artistic activities or craft work, going on retreats, engaging in pleasurable creative activities with friends or in solitude, performing compassionate work, and other revitalizing activities.

Kierkegaard pointed out long ago that "the ear is the most spiritually determined of the senses." Listening is fostered by the spiritually enriched and cared-for life. The life of the self is like a garden—"as ye sow, so shall ye reap." Sowing the seeds of "peace of mind" is an active process that persists throughout one's life and can be done every day. Building peace of mind is a good example of what is meant by "self-creation."

Mental tools that support listening

So far I have written mostly about the attitude and inner peace that make dialogical listening possible. In this section, I will describe a number of mental (language) tools that are part of the capacity to listen. The use of each one of these tools will help to get the work of listening done. A large number of linguistic devices can be used to support good listening. Fifteen language tools support dialogical listening:

1. Reiteration and describing what is heard

In a counselling conversation, one tool that the counsellor can use to ensure that he or she is receiving the meaning that the speaker is sending is to reiterate what the speaker has said. This takes the form of a paraphrase, a short phrase or sentence, or occasionally, a lengthier summary of what has been heard so far. A skilful listener can often use one key word to catch the essential meaning of what the help-seeker has said.

Help-seeker: "I have been trying to get my mother to consider going into a care home, since she has fallen many times lately and I am worried that she will fall and not be able to get up by herself. She might just lie there and die. But she will not hear of moving."

Helper: "You are afraid that your mother will fall and won't be able to get up or get help for herself, but she won't listen to you."

Helper 2: "That your mom might fall, and not be able to get help, and yet won't consider moving to a care home is a big worry to you."

Reiterations should be short and natural sounding, accurately reflect the meaning of what the person has said, and be *descriptive*, not interpretive.

2. Use of concrete images

It is important to use concrete examples and metaphors, especially when reiterating. For example:

"You are up against a wall."

"You are ready to stay in for the long haul."

"Getting that job was like striking gold."

For many people concrete expressions that are common in everyday speech are able to convey meaning much better than technical, abstract, or professional terms.

3. Questions that seek to clarify

Questions that *clarify* the meaning of what the speaker is expressing support dialogical listening. The questioner must refrain from asking leading questions, and not allow his or her own assumptions to shape the actual question. Examples of questions designed to clarify are:

"What do you mean by that?"
"What is another way of saying that?"
"Can you give an example of that?"
"How does that work?"
"Where did that take place?"

4. Questions that seek descriptions—not speculations

A help-seeker may speak in a way that confuses the distinction between what he or she has actually experienced and subsequent theorizing or speculating about what was experienced. For example:

"When I was coming home in the car I felt quite worried about my job interview. *I guess I have a low self-esteem.*"

The first sentence is a description of experience. The second ("I guess I have a low self-esteem") is a theorizing or speculative statement.

While there may be a place for theorizing about the reasons for experience, it is more important to encourage the descriptions and re-descriptions of actual experience. This is in keeping with Burke's[40] dramatistic method of analyzing an "act/situation." He suggests that five terms—act, agent, agency, scene, and purpose—are the mental tools needed to analyze virtually all human situations in which there is concern about what people are doing and why. Five questions guide the process of eliciting descriptions of the problem and call for careful listening:

59

Act—What is the action or activity that is creating concern? (This should be a description of what is actually going on, not a speculation about why it is going on.)
Basic question: What is happening?
Agent—Who is doing the acting?
Basic question: Who is doing what?
Agency—What means are being used by the actor(s)?
Basic question: How is the activity being done?
Scene—What is the situation or context in which the action is taking place?
Basic question: Where is this happening and what are the particulars of the context?
Purpose—What purpose is being served by these acts? (This element can be speculative, but it can also be a description.)
Basic question: What goal do the actor(s) wish to achieve?

Burke's contention is that in any given circumstance—especially those in which there is a question of motive—there must be some kind of answer to each of these five questions. This type of pentadic analysis has been in use for centuries. It is a way of organizing descriptions of experience so that a motive and/or problematic situation and action can be understood with minimal imposition of the observer's interpretations.

5. Questions that generate meaning

Constructive, generative dialogue is a way to create and describe meaning. In conversations with others, we can support the meaning-making process by asking certain kinds of questions and refraining from asking other kinds. Preferred questions are those that focus on meaning and not explanation. For example:

"*What* does that mean to you?" not "*Why* is that important to you?"

"*How* does that work?" not, "*Why* does that work?"

"*What* is it about your relationships at work that seem really important to you?"

"*How* is this incident different from the one you had last week?

60

Meaning-generating questions and description-eliciting questions are often similar.

6. *Self-observation and control of internal responses*

Upon hearing messages carrying strong feelings, such as feelings of misery and suffering, feelings of anger and hostility, or feelings of sadness and loss, a helper will often not be aware of her own internal response to what she hears. This can lead to fear, in the case of hearing hostility, or sympathy, in the case of hearing of suffering or sadness. Such internal reactions can cloud the perceptions of the helper and give rise to responses that interfere with, or impose upon, the speaker's expressed meaning. For example, upon hearing a sad story, the helper may feel sympathy and identify with the sad state of the other.

This is not to say that the counsellor should be unfeeling. Rather, the counsellor should be aware of his or her internal response, keep a clear distinction between self and other, and then be in a better position to make a more useful reply. It is possible to convey to another that you understand their feelings, how difficult it must be for them to have those feelings, and the circumstances giving rise to the feelings, and yet not be drawn into the sadness or feelings of misery that the other is expressing. One can learn to maintain an internal objectivity toward oneself and at the same time remain open and receptive to hearing what the other has to say. Much of what is called "burn-out" results from helpers not being able to self-observe and keep a clear distinction between self and other.

Self-observation is also essential in order to keep track of the process of communication and the part you are playing in it, as indicated by the next two tools. The skill of self-observation can be developed only by conscious effort on the part of the individual and is a life-long undertaking. A low capacity to self-observe almost always results in less than adequate listening.

7. *Conscious turn-taking in conversation*

Conversation is a series of speaking and listening episodes between two persons. In everyday conversation, neither partner in the conversation may even be aware of the communication process. They may talk over each other, dominate the talking time,

61

do very little listening, and just barely keep any conversation going.

In counselling conversations, it is the responsibility of the helper (as a guide in the communication process) to remain aware of turn taking. This means refraining from interrupting the other, promoting listening as well as speaking, and playing a reciprocating role in the conversation. Most novice counsellors talk far more than is necessary or desirable in counselling conversations.

As a rule of thumb, the counsellor should use about thirty per cent of the time speaking and the rest of the time in a listening mode. Of course many factors bear on this ratio—ability, willingness of the help-seeker to express herself, cultural compatibility, safety of the counselling space, and so on.

8. Conscious topic change announcements

Many ordinary conversations sound like a ping-pong game. Neither partner seems to pay very much attention to what the other has said. Jumping from one topic or story to another makes for a discontinuity of meaning. Other conversationalists are highly competitive, with each participant bringing up a new topic each time he speaks.

It is also common to observe conversations in which one, or sometimes both, partners seem determined to control what is being talked about. They will keep control of the conversation by asking questions on topics they wish to have discussed, or will interrupt the other, or tell long stories that keep the door closed to the other participant in the conversation.

Helpers have a responsibility to promote a more purposive, thoughtful conversation. One way to do this is to remain aware of the topic under discussion and not bring up another topic without first checking if the other has anything more to say. This awareness of topic change is called meta-communication and is a mark of an effective conversationalist. For example, when a topic in the conversation has been explored and the helper wishes to introduce another topic, she might say something like:

"You have been telling me about your experience with your teacher in class. I would like to change our discussion and talk about what kind of interaction you have with your teacher outside the class. *How does this shift seem to you?"*

Provided the help-seeker appears ready to change topics and does not have more to say about her in-class experience, then the helper starts on the new topic. This may seem a bit awkward. However, after one becomes aware of topic changing, it is fairly easy to announce topic changes in a natural way.

9. Listening for what is experienced

SocioDynamic counselling proceeds by trying to elicit, clarify, describe, and understand how the other is experiencing his or her concern. This means that the counsellor should approach the help-seeker in ways that address the following questions:

- What has actually been going on for you?
- What do you think about your situation?
- How do you feel about what has happened?
- What thoughts do you have about what to do next?
- When you reflect on what has happened, what are the most important parts of the situation to you?

The main guiding point for the counsellor is to give high priority to the *description of experience, situations, actions, and perceptions* and to hold in abeyance impulses to ask for reasons, justifications, causes, speculations, and theories about what has happened and why. Once there is a clear description in hand, any theory developed of possible reasons and explanations will have a much better chance of being relevant and helpful to both helper and help-seeker.

Sometimes the clarity that comes with describing and re-describing will in itself be the resolving force. In a sense, the problem simply disappears when it is seen without the fog of abstraction. On the other hand, a good explanation (theory) may be extremely helpful, once the nature of the concern has been made lucid through description.

10. Recognizing the two levels of all messages
In conversations, each message carries two types of meaning:

1. Informational content. Interpersonal messages carry the information that the speaker wishes to convey.
2. Relational meaning. Interpersonal messages carry a relational meaning.

A good maxim is: It is not just *what* you say that counts, but also *how* you say it. Consider the simple request, "Close the door." The informational message is quite straightforward. However, depending upon the tone of voice used by the speaker, or the inflection, the utterance can have many different meanings. It can mean criticism for leaving the door open. It may convey helpfulness, if it is a matter-of-fact statement about what to do next. It may suggest intimacy, as when one lover says to the other, "Close the door of the bedroom." And so on.

Quite often the tone of voice is a message about status, as in "I am in charge here." The relational message may also convey subtleties, such as ambivalence, distrust, respect, care, indifference, interest, criticism, approval, and countless other interpersonal messages. The important point is that any interpersonal message can, and usually does, have two types of meaning. The relational message is often the most important. It will have the effect of supporting or curtailing open communication between conversationalists.

11. Understanding and valuing silence
Many counsellors say that they feel uncomfortable in the face of silence on the part of the help-seeker. In response to their own uneasiness, they often "fill in" the empty space with their own questions and talk. There are various kinds of silence, ranging from the silence of hostility to the silence of adoration. In helping conversations, however, it can be assumed that there are two main reasons for silence on the help-seeker's part. Either the person does not know *what* to say or *how* to say it, or believes that it is unsafe or unwise to voice what she is thinking or feeling.

64

While there is no foolproof formula to guide the helper on how to respond to silence, certain ideas can help. For example, if it seems to be a matter of not knowing what to say rather than a matter of safety, then the helper can keep in mind the following:

- Often silence indicates that the speaker is thinking things over in her own mind and is considering the possible ways she can respond. This is especially true in intercultural conversations. For the helper to break into the other's reflections by asking a question, or by prompting the help-seeker to "go on," amounts to a disruption of the other's thought processes. It can also be taken as a sign of disapproval and disrespect. It is usually best for the counsellor to wait and let the help-seeker begin speaking when she is ready to do so.
- Falling silent can mean that the other is inwardly reviewing what has already been said in the conversation and is building up a mental context from which to speak. Silence may also mean that the help-seeker is sorting out conflicts or disturbances in how she thinks about the topic under discussion. Again, acceptant waiting is usually better than quizzing or trying to get the other to speak before she is ready to.
- In those instances in which the silence occurs because the speaker feels unsafe, then the counsellor can take steps to make the communication environment more safe and protected.

Feeling unsafe may arise from many conditions:

- There are intrusions and distractions in the counselling meeting place.
- The help-seeker may feel in jeopardy if she reveals certain information or, conversely, if she does not reveal information.
- The help-seeker may not understand the nature of counselling.

- The counsellor may have neglected to explain the conditions of confidentiality for counselling.
- The counsellor may present himself as overbearing, officious or interrogative, or may be moving the conversation too swiftly for the help-seeker's comfort.

Of course, there are many times when the counsellor should pay attention to silence and investigate the help-seeker's reasons for being silent. This can be done in a respectful manner. For example, by saying something like, "I notice that you are quiet. I am wondering what you are thinking about."

The extra-lingual signs that accompany silence should not escape the observant helper. The "look" on the help-seeker's face, changing of posture, movements of the help-seeker's hands, tearing in the eyes, aversion or fixing of gaze—all such non-verbal signs may signal that the other needs respectful acceptance. Or these signals can mean that the help-seeker needs help in saying what she is thinking or feeling, or needs to feel safer and less at-risk.

12. Listening for different voices

The autobiographical self is constructed by individuals as they learn to give voice to different streams of experience, for example, learning through experience what it means to be a man or woman, a bookkeeper, a baker, a truck driver, or an artist. Each stream of experience gives rise to a voice. So a person can speak as a husband, cook, gardener, poet, soccer player, merchant, and so on. A self is not just a single voice; it is composed of multiple voices. When a person seeks help, the helper should be attuned to, and listen for, the voice or voices that the help-seeker uses in the conversation. What status is being signalled by the voice of the help-seeker? That of "boss," "helpless person," "child," "adult," "accuser," "one-on-the-margin," or countless others? Each voice emerges from a frame of experience that is used to interpret what is happening from that person's view of himself or herself at any given point in time. Voices are always telling the story of a particular self.

13. *Listening for that which is beyond the spoken*

When we listen to another, we must try to remember that behind the person speaking face-to-face with us in this moment, there is a unique biography and set of remembered experiences. These mark the path of a help-seeker's travels and the ways they have made their way through time and different contexts.

When we listen to another's utterances, we are trying to grasp the phenomenon they are revealing to us in the immediate present. We wish to discern what they mean by their words. Sometimes this is a rather straightforward matter; that is, the meaning of what is said is clear to us and we need not wonder about what is not being said.

However, it is important to remember that within any phenomenon, spoken words or actions manifest in various ways and may be "covered up." The meaning of any particular object, idea, experience, or other phenomena may be covered up[41] in the following ways:

- It can be *disguised* (it is not what it seems to be on first glance—for example, a laugh that might seem to be a sign of humour is, instead, a sign of nervousness).
- It can be *undiscovered,* in the sense that it is neither known or unknown (whatever is presenting itself is just not recognized and remains unnoticed—we are unaware that we do not know).
- It can be *buried* (it has been known or recognized sometime, but it has been lost and covered over by other meanings).

The helper who is listening carefully to what the other is saying can begin to enjoy the experience of listening deeply by using an open-minded grasping of the meanings that are revealed.

The skilful listener keeps in mind that what the help-seeker is expressing may be only *a part* of her concern/problem. There may be a wealth of meanings that are relevant to her concern and potentially could be expressed but are not. There are many reasons why a person may not articulate fully their thoughts, feelings, and perceptions: nervousness, fear, lack of prior experience in expressing self, concern with privacy, failed memory, cautiousness, or uncertainty about the reliability of the counsellor, for example.

The counsellor's questions should not have a "prying" motive. However, the counsellor should be aware that the help-seeker may be choosing to ignore, or may be unable to express, certain issues.

Meaning often gets covered up in an accidental way, even when there is no intention on the other's part to disguise the communication. Whatever the reasons for undisclosed meaning, the skilful listener will catch glimpses of disguised, undiscovered, and buried-over meaning. By gently calling these glimpses to the attention of the speaker, a much fuller revelation of meaning may be made.

It is important to use metaphors as a way of letting different meanings become known. The meaning of *metaphor* itself is to "transport beyond," for example, a counsellor may say to a help-seeker:

"The way you describe your problem makes it sound like a puzzle with missing pieces. I wonder if it seems that way to you?"

The puzzle metaphor may prompt the help-seeker to search for missing pieces of her story.

14. Using mapping to expand listening

Mapping is a method of visualizing and making a drawing of what is being discussed. The counsellor and help-seeker cooperatively make a "map" of the experience or concern with which the help-seeker wishes to be helped. The drawing process and the dialogue of the counselling conversation go hand in hand. By listening carefully to what the help-seeker is saying as she visualizes her concern, and by asking questions that establish different dimensions or spheres of meaning in the map, both counsellor and help-seeker expand their understandings of the concern.

15. *Cultural codes and object-mediated listening*

Differences in cultural membership influence the understandings that counsellor and help-seeker can achieve in the counselling process. The SocioDynamic perspective suggests that while language differences can hinder understanding, the most important factor is the counsellor's attitude as a listener, especially attitudes of respect and open-mindedness and the *ability to learn cultural rules and codes from help-seekers.*

Every culture has specific codes to govern communication, especially interpersonal communication. For example, in some cultures, hand shaking is an important gesture of the desire to communicate; in other cultures, the practice of hand shaking does not exist. Western cultures tend to emphasize gaze and eye contact as important features of interpersonal communication. In other cultures, direct eye contact is interpreted as aggressive and a violation of personal space.

The cultural context, cultural codes about how communication should be done, and the cultural tools that both counsellor and help-seeker bring to the counselling meeting are factors that influence what the help-seeker is willing to say, how the counsellor listens, and what the counsellor is prepared to hear.

The counsellor who wishes to improve listening and make communication more effective with culturally different help-seekers can take the position of "not-knowing" and permit himself to learn from members of the other culture the rules that govern conversation in that culture. For example, in a first-time meeting between counsellor and help-seeker, if the counsellor is a female and the help-seeker is an Arab male immigrant, the conversation may be quite difficult. This interpersonal situation of male and female strangers speaking with each other in a private conversation breaks an important cultural code in Arab culture.

One of the best ways to learn about cultural codes is to arrange to have conversations with members of another culture who have already become familiar with the customs of the culture of the counsellor. In such a conversation, the counsellor can ask questions about what to do and what not to do, and what to expect in a conversation. This type of learning from others can help counsellors to avoid obvious "mistakes" in communicating with immigrants, refugees, and other persons coming from cultures other than the counsellor's own.

There are times when cultural objects can be used to foster communication and to improve listening. I remember the first time I was responsible for helping some Greek immigrants adapt to life in a new culture. Several of the men who spoke English would keep fingering beads as we talked. At first I had no idea what they were doing, or why. Finally, I asked one of the men what these beads meant to him and what he was doing with them. He laughed and said that they were "prayer" beads. I asked him if he was praying while we talked. He laughed again and said, "No, they keep me from feeling nervous when we talk." We then talked about different types of prayer beads and their functions in different situations. This is an example of *object-mediated* communication. Knowing about the cultural significance of the prayer beads enabled me to listen to the speaker with a different and more expanded perspective.

In addition to these fifteen mental tools for supporting listening, one further consideration is the provision of a meeting environment that is relatively free of distracting influences. It is very difficult to maintain close attention to another when distractions are occurring. Environment-related distractions to be avoided include other people walking by or through the listening space, the ringing of a telephone, loud-speaker announcements, intrusion by colleagues or other staff, sunlight in the eyes, or an uncomfortable, dirty, or dreary meeting place. The extent to which the counsellor is able to protect listening by providing a listening-friendly environment is a test of the respect that the counsellor shows helpseekers.

Harmonious relations support listening

Communication occurs in the context of a relationship. We use communication to build relationships, and we use relationships to facilitate communication. To *harmonize* means to bring the parts of a whole into accord. It means to bring together the component parts

70

of a system or process so that they resonate with each other. In interpersonal contexts such as counselling, harmony can refer to both inner peace and calm and to interpersonal relationships.

If listening is to be really effective, then relations between listener and speaker must be in some degree of harmony, rather than discord. Listening should have the quality of whole attention, which should not be broken by distractions and inattentiveness.

What are some of the features of harmonious relation in the counselling process, and how do they contribute to listening? At the start of counselling, the helper can exercise a degree of control over how the counselling communication and process unfolds. A competent counsellor will try to "set the stage" for constructive exchanges and problem solving by establishing an atmosphere of harmony and support with the help-seeker.

Effective counsellors know the importance of finding or creating *common ground*, even with help-seekers who are very different from themselves. A counsellor may also need to explain the purpose of counselling to the help-seeker, since many first-time help-seekers either have no conception of counselling or else have a misleading idea of counselling.

A good counsellor also knows that it is often not a good idea to direct attention too quickly to the concern of the help-seeker. A good maxim to follow when beginning counselling is *listen to relate* first, *listen to problem solve* second. In this way a resonant, harmonious climate for the counselling can be established as a relational context for pursuing the goals of the help-seeker.

The tools that good counsellors have at hand to promote harmony are

- Capacity for self-observation—this can enable the counsellor to reduce interference in her own ability to listen. This means to use self-observation to reduce the distracting intrusion of inner responses, such as prejudice, bias, fear, dislike, sympathy, identification, stress, and resentment, into her own perception of the other and of the counselling process. This enables her to remain "present to" the speaker.

71

- Recognition of the readiness of the help-seeker for counselling. Many counselling encounters fail because the help-seeker is not in a ready state of mind for the counselling conversation.
- Attitude of respect for the help-seeker and for the help-seeker's concern. Conveying respect for the other is an essential condition of almost all aspects of the counselling process.
- Commitment to the value of joint action,
- Openness to learning from the help-seeker,
- A commitment to the principle of "many possibilities,"
- Capacity to be a guide in the "constructive present," and
- Ability to create a communication environment that is safe, trustworthy, and conducive to transformative learning.

Given these features, the counsellor can present a human face that reflects inward calmness, concentration, care, and responsibility for those parts of the help-seeker's life that are placed before her.

The counsellor can encourage harmonious relations by coming to the counselling situation as an inwardly harmonized person, by initiating communication that is intended to be helpful (regardless of the help-seeker's initial desire and capacity for interpersonal communication), and by guiding the help-seeker's participation in counselling activities that are organized within the "constructive present."

As counselling proceeds, the use of dialogical communication adjusted to the social location and cultural membership of the help-seeker will promote harmonious relations between counsellor and help-seeker. Harmony tends to produce conversation to which it is worth listening.

Transformative learning
Dialogical listening is an excellent tool for creating an environment that is conducive to transformative learning. Transformation theory implies an active process of recognizing and reinterpreting previously learned knowledge so that it makes sense in a new context.

72

Transformative learning is not just memorization, nor mere accumulation of knowledge, nor is it simple association of the old and new. Transformative learning implies that new meanings, new interpretations, and new understandings result from learning experiences.

In transformative learning, the learner's perspective changes. This does not imply that the help-seeker merely adjusts to or passively accepts a constraining force or situation. In fact, a new perspective is often the key event in moving forward and establishing control over some aspect of the context or existential situation that was previously perceived as insurmountable, or that just had to be passively accepted.

I remember a young woman who came to me for counselling regarding how she might prepare herself to find employment. As I listened to her story, it became clear to me that she was in an abusive relationship with a man. At first, she spoke of this condition as "normal." She had witnessed abuse in her sisters' and her mother's relationships with men. Her perspective was that this was "the way it is supposed to be."

We discussed her experience and what she wanted from life. I also suggested that she attend group counselling at the Women's Centre, where counselling groups for abused women were conducted. She did join the group and continued to meet with me from time to time. As she listened to the stories of other women about the abuse in their lives, and what some of them were doing to rid themselves of abusive relationships, she began to perceive her own situation differently—she no longer considered her circumstances as normal but as unacceptable. With a change in perspective, she was able to act in ways to extricate herself from abuse.

The point I am making is that the first step was for me to listen carefully as she expressed her experience. Then she listened to other women with whom she had common ground tell their stories of abuse and their reactions to abusive situations. She also learned of other sources of support for herself in any efforts she might make to improve her life situation. The key activities in the process of her transformation in perspective were listening—me listening to her stories and she to other women's stories—and being listened to.

One of the characteristics of dialogical listening is that the listener listens while at the same time keeping his or her own prior knowledge and interpretations and immediate reactions from blocking or changing the meaning of what the other is saying. The listener tries to understand what the other is saying before allowing his or her own reactions to come into play.

When both participants recognize an important difference and agree on the meaning of the topic, then they enter into a negotiation of the difference in opinion or perspective. So long as good will and the dialogical perspective are maintained, an understanding can develop that is, in some ways, new to both participants. The meanings of both have been transformed into new meanings or perspectives.

In this sense, thesis A and thesis B have been synthesized into (a new) thesis C. This does not mean that all differences are necessarily reconciled, rather it means that any genuine difference is much more clearly understood by both. It also means that one difference does not necessarily block a common understanding of other aspects of the topic under discussion. Another possible meaning might be that a fusion of the understandings of both participants leads to an entirely new and common understanding. In such a case, both participants have transformed perspectives; that is, they share a new perspective.

The dialogical listener enters into dialogue with a willingness to change, if presented with good reasons for so doing. In SocioDynamic counselling neither participant is regarded as an absolute authority, especially not an authority conferred by status. The authority of dialogue rests in the clarity, examination, evaluation, and goodness of ideas. It also arises from the ability to think together, to join the other in a partnered search for understanding through the exercise of undistorted listening, and the sincere exchange and examination of ideas, knowledge, and attitudes.

Transformative learning arises from a process of meaning making and not from a process of proving that one is right or knowing and the other is wrong or unknowing. Many theories of learning are based on the assumption that we take new experience and validate it using old criteria—applying the test of the "tried and true." Transformative learning tends to reverse this process. Interpretations of old experience are altered by new perceptions. Criteria for making evaluations of experience are not necessarily rooted in past learning. They can also arise from new experiences, from seeing that "things are not the way they used to be," and in understanding "how things are" and realizing that "they do not have to be that way."

To summarize, dialogical listening rests upon three conditions: peace of mind (freedom from distraction), harmonious relations (trust, respect, and support), and an orientation toward transformative learning (changed perspective). The counsellor has the responsibility for using and promoting dialogical listening. In some cases, the help-seeker will have no capacity or even interest in good listening. However, even under very difficult conditions, the counsellor can take any opportunity that is presented both to model dialogical listening and to encourage the other to enter into dialogue instead of arguing, demanding, or relating in a passive or helpless manner.

Everything comes down to the ear you are able to hear me with. Jacques Derrida[42]

Mindful Problem Solving
Mindlessness and mindful problem solving[43]

There are many models for problem solving. A model favoured in SocioDynamic helping is "mindful problem solving." Before describing how it works, I will first comment on mindlessness, a stark contrast to mindfulness. Mindlessness, as a state of mind, is one in which we repeat what we already know or know how to do in an automatic way. However, when confronted with unusual conditions, *repetitive responses* often are inadequate. The individual is simply saying or doing "what I always do," and this makes him or her blind to the need for innovation and changed perspective.

A second characteristic of mindlessness is *over-commitment* to one way of doing things or one idea about something. The person who is strongly committed to one way of thinking about something, will resist critical thinking and will tend to label other ideas as irrelevant or impractical.

Mindlessness is supported by a *belief in limited resources.* Any experienced counsellor will have heard many times statements like: "Nothing can be done," "There are no possibilities," "I just can't do anything about it," "There are no jobs anywhere," "Nothing works for me," "There is no money for that," and so on. Such comments convey a belief that there are no available resources, personal or otherwise. These are defeatist ideas that restrict critical and creative thinking and acting.

Submission to calendar time can be another aspect of mindlessness. This means that the person believes that we must abide by the clock and calendar and that time is completely governed by sources outside ourselves.

Single-minded pursuit of a single outcome predisposes one to mindlessness. A commitment to "outcomes" in work and also in social situations can induce mindlessness. If a person, instead of thinking, "Can I do this correctly?" or "Can I achieve this outcome or goal?" thinks instead, "How can I do this?" the emphasis is on the "how" of doing something, rather than whether it is done correctly or satisfies a goal. The effects, then, are to open a person's mind to various possibilities and multiple ways of proceeding and thus escape the "outcome trap."

De-contextualization also contributes to mindlessness. Often when trying to solve a problem, the person completely ignores the context in which the problem is arising, along with the context in which possible solutions can be made. Context confusion can also promote mindlessness, for example, when the counsellor forgets that the context within which she is considering the help-seeker's problem and the context in which the help-seeker is placing the problem may be very different. In this case, the ensuing conversation lacks any understanding, with both counsellor and help-seeker mindlessly repeating their own perspectives.

People often assume that actions taken by one person have the same motives, reasons, and results as similar actions taken by

76

another person. However, what is a failure in one context can be a success in another. The youth who takes drugs is making a terrible mistake as far as his parents are concerned. However, in the context of his peer group, he is scoring big and "showing the right stuff." If we wish to understand the reasons for another's actions, or absence of action, we need to be attuned to the context in which the other is living and use the other's actions and ideas as a frame of reference and source of meaning.

Counsellors often encounter help-seekers who seem to be unusually difficult to work with. At one extreme, they may present themselves as helpless and defeated. At the other extreme, they can be demanding, hostile, and uncooperative in many ways. Counselling literature is full of references to "resistant clients" and "helpless clients." However, the SocioDynamic perspective takes a somewhat different view. The SocioDynamic perspective asks, "What context or frame of mind is this person using to interpret his life situation?" Instead of using the vocabulary of resistance, help-seekers are perceived as being in a state of mind of either being ready or not ready for productive counselling. The help-seeker who is not ready for counselling presents the counsellor with the challenge of doing things that will prepare the help-seeker to *become ready* for productive counselling.

Self-perception of helplessness and ability to solve problems
Before proceeding to a discussion of mindfulness as a good strategy for promoting learning conditions in counselling, I will list some of the "symptoms" of the difficult or unready help-seeker. Whether passive or hostile, the help-seeker who frustrates the counsellor's overtures is almost always acting from a self-perception of helplessness, failure, and insecurity. The following are clues that a help-seeker is operating from a sense of insecurity and helplessness:

- Interprets the counsellor's comments as judgmental or incorrect.
- Has an automatic response: "That won't work."
- Demands that the counsellor "fix" the problem.

- Attempts to distract the counsellor by bringing up irrelevant issues or by meandering without focus in the conversation.
- Is preoccupied with "diagnosis" and often insists on being tested.
- Insists on a guaranteed outcome provided by the counsellor.
- Appears to have a need to "prove something" to the counsellor.
- Has a lengthy list of all the things that are wrong in his or her life.
- Frequently changes the subject.
- Tries to amuse or flatter the counsellor.
- Boasts of unrelated achievements or successes.
- Is fixed in black and white thinking (good and bad, right and wrong).
- Uses blaming and accusatory language and expresses the belief that someone else is to blame for his or her problems.
- Seeks assurance that he or she is doing better and often asks how he or she compares with others in similar circumstances.
- Keeps repeating ideas and actions that are not productive.
- Questions the competence of the helper.
- Shows "functional fixity" or "frozen categories," that is, believes that ideas, actions and objects have only one correct function.

Self-presentations such as these indicate that the help-seeker is too strongly attached to outcome goals, not able to concentrate, focussed on single ideas or actions, and generally, feeling threatened and vulnerable. These ways of presenting self also add up to a very restricted perspective and do not allow the help-seeker to entertain new possibilities. The individual is unable to risk expanding his or her own set of interpretations of what is happening and why.

The preceding discussions of mindlessness and the difficult client provide a context for a brief description of mindful problem solving as a counselling practice,

Mindfulness as a state of mind

Mindful problem solving arises from a particular *state of mind*, which is a configuration of thoughts and feelings (something like a mood) that can predispose the helper and/or help-seeker to act and interact in certain ways with other people. Heidegger[44] has pointed out that every mood has its understanding. The following discussion of mindful problem solving is a description of this state of mind and consequent actions stemming from it.

Generally, a mindful state is calm and focussed on the process of problem solving. It is reflective and balanced in affect. It is concentrated and attentive and in search of meaning and deepened understanding. It has a quality of patience. It is open to its own and another's experience. Finally, it is oriented to creative contributions to problem solving and open to dialogue with others. Being focussed on process means paying attention to (a) the realities of my existential situation, (b) my own thoughts and feelings about the constructive present and the interactive process in which I am engaged, and (c) how I can increase my "how-to" capacity for acting in this situation.

Six components of mindfulness

Langer suggests five components to mindfulness. I have made minor adaptations to these and I have added a further dimension— dialogue. I suggest that these six dimensions produce a state of mind that can be quite valuable for problem solving within the context of helping. The mindfulness components include:

1. Encouraging a *playful attitude* and experimenting with new ideas, categories, and ways of doing things.
2. Welcoming *new information* and trying to convert it to personal know-how. Just receiving information is not sufficient. In fact, it may only create confusion and feelings of inadequacy. Information must be digested, discussed, and given a place of meaning in an individual's life-space if it is to inform effectively decisions and actions.

79

3. Recognizing that there is *more than one way* of viewing things and any one thing can show itself in various ways. Recognizing that there are multiple views about nearly everything can be a liberating realization.
4. Taking steps to gain more *control over context*(s).
5. Giving *process* high priority. It helps to realize that a process precedes every outcome. Often attention to process will help ensure that an outcome is achieved at all and can affect the quality of the outcome as well.
6. Implementing the *dialogic principle in interpersonal communication* as much as possible. Most problems and solutions are constructed through dialogue and interaction. Since problem solving is frequently relational, then increasing the quality of interpersonal communication is essential to fruitful problem solving.

Mindful problem solving is a process that emphasizes awareness, reflection, and cooperation between helper and help-seeker.

Intelligent Conversation
From a SocioDynamic perspective, a core activity in helping is *intelligent conversation*. Intelligent conversation is a form of communication in which helper and help-seeker work together to describe and resolve the concerns brought to the counselling situation by the help-seeker. The counsellor does not speak with the voice of an expert who can fix problems using superior knowledge, skill, and values. Nor is there an assumption that the best solutions or resolutions are always lying in wait in the help-seeker and emerge if the counsellor is just patient and supportive. Intelligent conversation fosters the intelligence and creativity of both helper and help-seeker, actively bringing these to bear on the help-seeker's concern. Conversation is the means for co-producing shared understanding, insights, agreements, and plans for forward movement in the help-seeker's life.

There are several types of conversation. One type is everyday, mundane conversation just barely adequate to keep the communication going. Typically, participants in everyday communication are not aware of the communication process as such, or their part in it. They do not engage in meta-communication.

A second form of conversation heard in everyday encounters is "polite" conversation in which participants are guided by rules of etiquette and what it is polite to say in a particular situation. The main purpose of the conversation is to avoid saying offensive or hurtful comments and also to avoid controversy and conflict. Polite conversation is a carefully controlled form of conversation in which many thoughts and feeling are repressed and not expressed. Polite conversing invokes status distinctions based on such considerations as age, social location, gender, sex, family relations, institutional role, and class.

A third type of conversation is "authoritative" conversation in which one person dominates and controls the conversation on the basis of status, authority, expertise, or other forms of interpersonal power. Conversations between parent and child, prisoner and warden, teacher and pupil, boss and employee, physician and patient, are common examples of conversations in which one person is regarded as the authority and the other as of lesser status. The counselling or therapy "interview" is another form of controlled conversation, especially when the counsellor assumes the role of an expert, based on status.

In actual practice, a conversation may be a combination of polite, authoritative, and mundane depending upon who is conversing in what context and about what. However, none of these three types of conversation is a desirable model for counselling.

A fourth type of conversation is *intelligent conversation,* which is structured to promote the best use of intelligence and creativity on the part of both participants. Intelligent conversation is composed of four interactive elements: dialogue, problem solving, meta-communication, and an attitude of respect. Help-seekers may or may not know how to participate in intelligent conversation; the counsellor-as-model will typically influence them to move in the direction of dialogue.

In *intelligent conversation* are found the following characteristics:

1. The *dialogical principle* is used in an effort to insure that meaning flows both ways.
2. A *commitment* to a problem-solving attitude is evident.
3. Also evident is an ability to *meta-communicate* (comment on the communication).
4. An attitude of *respect* for the uniqueness and moral worth of the other is shown, although there may be clear differences of opinion, perspective, value, and patterns of action demonstrated (love the sinner, not the sin).
5. Participants show a *desire to co-produce* the conversation and avoid domination and control of one by the other.
6. *Personal experience* is respected, validated, and regarded as an extremely important source of knowledge.
7. Ability to engage in *interpersonal negotiation* is manifest. Plans and agreements are arrived at through a process of interpersonal negotiation and not by fiat.
8. The conversation is characterized by *supportiveness*, rather than indifference or outright destructiveness; *self-responsibility*, rather than accusation; *intention to understand*, rather than proving oneself correct; *openness*, rather than defensiveness; and *inclusion* rather than exclusion.
9. Participants are open to the idea of *multiple realities*. Intelligent conversation assumes that both counsellor and help-seeker have important contributions to make to the counselling process. It is also assumed that the help-seeker is potentially an active, creative agent capable of intelligent thinking.

Figure 3. Life-Space Map of Help-Seeker's Problem.

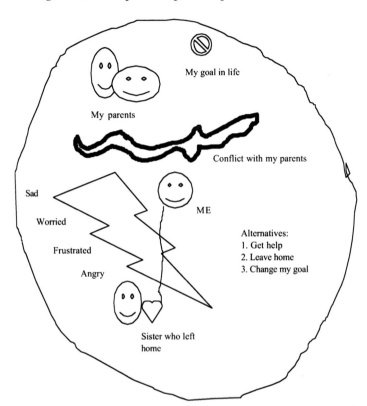

Visualization and Life-Space Mapping

In the life-space map shown in Figure 3, a seventeen-year-old help-seeker has mapped her problem. Her parents are opposed to her following her plan for a future, which was to become a volunteer overseas peace program worker. She is angry, sad, frustrated, and worried. She and her counsellor have listed three alternatives at this point. She has a twenty-two-year-old sister who left home earlier because of conflict with the parents. She feels close to her sister, as she indicated by drawing a heart.

The counsellor guides the help-seeker's participation in making the map by making suggestions, such as:

- On this large piece of paper, we can make a map of what you are concerned about. Draw a big circle and put yourself in it (use a stick figure or just make an X).
- It is best if the help-seeker does the mapping under the guiding questions of the helper, or it can be a cooperative project. Occasionally, the helper must do the mapping because the help-seeker is unable to.
- After the circle and person have been drawn, then say, "This is your life-space (personal world) (present situation)." Then ask questions that will prompt the help-seeker to place features of his or her concern along with various contextual observations in the map. For example:
  - Who else, if anyone, is involved in your concern? Show them on your map.
  - When you think of your problem, what are some of the details that come into your mind? Encourage the help-seeker to use lines, images, colours, words, sentences, and symbols to put into visual form the feelings, thoughts, actions and situational details that seem to have meaning in relation to his or her life-space concern.
  - The counsellor should not make abstract, theoretical interpretations of what is mapped. The map is an attempt to articulate and describe what is actually happening in the person's life experience. The purpose of life-space mapping is to elicit a description of experience, not theoretical interpretation.

Mapping and dialogue go hand-in-hand and each can contribute to the meaning produced by the other. Frequently, there will be several maps constructed during a single counselling conversation. Mapping has many valuable functions:

- Clarifying and simplifying complex circumstances.
- Creating new insights and ideas about the concern.
- Identifying strengths and identifying barriers.
- Serving as a preliminary plan for action.

84

- Revealing influences and patterns in the help-seeker's situation.
- Revealing important relationships and connections.
- Making the self visible.
- Revealing the help-seeker's sense of self within the existential realities at hand.
- Producing important descriptions of actions, feelings, and interactions.
- Contextualizing the concern.

While mapping may not be done in every counselling session, it is an extremely important tool, when used effectively, for externalizing the help-seeker's life-space. A map is an excellent tool for creating a future and planning on how to move toward that future.

Co-Constructing Personal Projects

Jean-Paul Sartre wrote, "Through your *acts* you create yourself." Alain Touraine[45] asserted that human agency is defined through *acts and relations*. Lev Vygotsky advocated that *learning through doing* is preferable to learning by being told. Timo Vähämöttönen[46] proposed an *activity-based* counselling method within which counsellor and help-seekers negotiate their meanings and actions.

The SocioDynamic perspective emphasizes that counselling should assist help-seekers to engage in *meaningful personal activity projects* that increase capacity and strengthen self-identity. What is a personally meaningful activity project? "Activity" is used broadly to mean any set of actions ranging from simple activities, such as making a list or learning new words, to more complex activities, such as cooking food or using a computer to access the Internet, to very complex activities, such as managing a company or doing chemical analyses. The term *project* is used to emphasize that an activity is done to produce a product or accomplish a desired goal or task. A project usually implies construction, doing, or making. Anthony Giddens[47] wrote of the "self-as-project," meaning that we construct our selves. "Personally

85

meaningful" means that the person feels ownership of the project, "This is *my* project." The person may value the actual activity in itself or the hoped-for outcome, or both.

As used in the SocioDynamic perspective, a project is not prescribed or supplied to the help-seeker by the helper. It is agreed-upon by both as a worthwhile activity, often created by both, and is an activity about which the help-seeker says, in essence, "This activity makes sense to me; I can see how it is part of the process I am committed to; and I feel that I am both the maker and the implementer of this activity (project). Doing this project is a meaningful activity for me. If necessary, I am willing to put aside some other things in my life in order to do this project."

Ivan is a forty-year-old telephone operator. His marriage broke up; his daughter was in trouble in school; and Ivan became depressed and stressed about his job and finances. He met several times with a counsellor. After constructing a map that produced a clarified picture of Ivan's existential realities, he and his counsellor discussed and identified activities that would help him move back into a more secure feeling in his life. The projects that they agreed on were:

- To arrange a meeting with his supervisor and explain that he was not feeling up to par and request a change of shifts until his emotional health improved.
- To take a weekly swim at the recreation centre. He had been a regular swimmer prior to the onset of his troubles. He had stopped because he "just did not feel like it." After discussion, he decided that if it had been enjoyable before, it was worth taking up again.
- To write a letter to his best friend explaining what he was dealing with, and how.
- To consult with his physician.

Ivan found each of these activities to be sensible and worth doing. In the two weeks following the first counselling session, Ivan initiated each of his personal activity projects, and he told his counsellor that doing the projects had given give him a "window of hope."

Guidelines for co-constructing personal activity projects include:

1. Work together, pool knowledge and experience.
2. Keep the project at a low level of complexity.
3. Promote a "try this and see how it works out" attitude.
4. Confirm that the help-seeker *knows how to do* the activity; a person will only do what he or she knows how to do.
5. Try to make the project a "path of small steps."
6. Agree on a debriefing session to talk over and evaluate progress and make changes if necessary. Emphasize reconstruction rather than mistakes or failure.
7. Provide encouragement and keep clear who is responsible for what in regards to implementing the project.
8. Projects are a matter of "best guess" and should not be approached in an overly logical and "technical" manner.
9. Use mapping of the existential realities of the help-seeker's situation or concern within his or her life-space. Keep the project tied closely to these existential realities. Successful projects can often strengthen self-esteem, and build capacity. *How* the project is done is often as important as *what* gets done. Motivation lies in the process of making meaning and the experience of meaningfulness.

Remember that many solutions to problems are temporary, as indeed are many problems. There is always more than one way to conceive of a project and often several ways to carry them out. Invent, experiment, and revise are good guidelines in forming and doing personal activity projects. Creating and engaging in personal projects provide excellent examples of guided participation and joint action.

Guided Participation

I have taken the term *guided participation* from the work of the anthropologist Barbara Rogoff.[48] The term refers to communication and coordinated efforts between people as they co-participate in culturally valued activities. Guided participation refers to both hands-on activity and observation of others performing tasks that they wish to learn. The "guidance" comes from sharing commonly desired values, interaction with a respected and trusted social partner, and the observing and doing of activities. These are usually activities that the more experienced social partner (helper) values and in which she or he has experience and possesses greater competency and/or knowledge than the help-seeker.

Guided participation is a process and a situation of learning within which the individual personally appropriates know-how that can be used to handle subsequent situations. Through this process of guided participation, the individual may change in terms of capacity, values, perspective, or cultural habits. Thus it is a *process of becoming* more than a process of acquisition.

Mapping, intelligent conversation, cooperative counselling sessions, and activity based group sessions provide excellent opportunities for learning by guided participation. Counselling conducted as a cooperative process is a complex form of guided participation. The counsellor guides the help-seeker in the communication process, and the help-seeker guides the helper in the details of her life-space. Guided participation does not depend upon telling or prescribing. It is an interactive process of appropriation.

Transformative learning and guided participation are closely associated concepts. Transformative learning refers to learning through reflection resulting in a change in the individual's assumptions, perspectives, or ways of acting. In other words, transformative learning is not simply acquisition of information, knowledge, or skill. It *transforms* the individual from one state of being to another, or one capacity to another. For example, when a help-seeker, after several counselling sessions with her counsellor, says, "I no longer have the same idea for my future. I now see in a different way who I am and what I can do. I feel like a different person," this help-seeker is describing a transformative learning experience.

As already described, guided participation is a learning process that facilitates transformative learning. Individuals learn alongside another person or persons, through activity, not through

being told or prescribed to. This is learning in part through observation and in part through guided activity and imitation. The
SocioDynamic counsellor arranges learning conditions within the
counselling situation that enable the help-seeker to engage in transformative learning.

Future-Building

Within the SocioDynamic perspective, the concept of a "possible future" is quite significant and has a number of features. A
"future" is not a place, existing "out there" already. It is not waiting for us to arrive. In one sense, any idea of future is illusory
since there is nothing happening there yet. However, the idea of a
future has enormous power to create human movement. The ideas
that individuals have about futures can either empower or
disempower.

Sometimes it takes great effort to bring that future about; other
times a possible future becomes apparent almost as an accident.
Some futures we speculate about can fill us with dread; others fill
us with expectation of a better life, or even bliss. How we think
about futures can have an undeniable impact on how we conduct
ourselves in the present situation. The idea of future helps us to
"throw ourselves" or "project" ourselves toward an imagined life
course.

SocioDynamic thinking takes a three-part view of the idea of
future as it applies to the counselling process and about how future-building is conducted within the life-space of the person:

1. One must *imagine* a future. If an individual cannot imagine a particular future, the fundamental opportunity for
   achieving that particular future is missing,
2. If the future is one that the individual can imagine and is
   in the realm of possibility, then the individual must *desire*
   it. To "desire" means to endow it with personal meaning
   and to feel ready to engage in actions and projects that
   build the future into a here-and-now reality.
3. If a person can imagine a future and desires it, then the
   individual must *act* by doing those activities and projects

that, in effect, contribute to, or make, the future that is desired.

Futures, be they on the level of the individual or on the level of social or cultural groups, are always under construction and reconstruction. Futures are made or built. They are not "out there" waiting for us to arrive. A constructive present contains many rich, inspiring, and realistic images of futures that a person can consider, choose from, and act to create.

Futures are not predictable; they are always a matter of the "best guess." Of course, there are occasions when future-building events seem to "just happen" or seem to be accidental. We should always remain open to such possibilities, but for the vast majority of people, over most of their lives, the futures they experience, both good and bad, will be those they imagine, desire, and act to create.

Of course, there must be an *opportunity* for a future to be built. One cannot construct a future as a fully employed steelworker in an economy in which there are no opportunities for employment. In other words, we must be realistic in building futures. However, the counsellor should exercise great caution in advising a person that a possible future is unrealistic. This is very hard to determine. The world is full of people who did not fulfil their potentials because they were persuaded that some future they had desired was "not realistic." From time to time, one runs into an individual whom no one would have predicted could have realized the future that, in fact, was transformed from imagination into actuality by that particular person.

It also should be kept in mind that opinions about what is considered "realistic" are often more a function of the values and personal experience of the helper than anything else. Certainly, real constraints exist. However, many people, including counsellors, err on the side of a much too conservative attitude concerning what is "realistic" for help-seekers in their attempts to construct desired futures.

90

Self-Authoring

The self-authoring strategy is based on the ideas of Mikhail Bakhtin[49] and forms the conceptual basis for literary work to become a model for the construction and reconstruction of self. From the point of view of self-authoring, what is sought are the meanings of texts—both oral and written. The speaking and writing person produces "texts" that constitute the self. Thus we can employ the ideas of the "autobiographical self" and the "narrated self." Instead of trying to derive the forms of human conduct and the nature of the self from neurological and behavioural processes, the self is conceived as a symbolic-linguistic construction.

Consider the case, for example, of an individual who experiences a certain element of social life—for example, cooking—over a period of several years. The individual develops an ability to give voice to the various stories and meanings of cooking. What she is voicing—that is, her "oral texts"—enables her to say, "I am a cook," or "I can cook." She has, through experience, reached a point where she can narrate her self in these terms. She is able to give voice to and has authored her self-as-cook. This same process can be applied to a range of social life processes. The basic process is one in which personal experience leads to interpreted meaning, which in turn, leads to the ability to voice these meanings as storied aspect of self.

Several self-authoring procedures make up this self-authoring strategy. These strategies are based on the assumption that it is valuable to the help-seeker to gain deepened understanding of how she or he "makes" or constructs his or her self though various activities. This understanding arises from the recognition that a person's self is authored and that the stories that a person narrates are indicators of who that person is. When a person tells the helper her story of losing a job and the consequences of this experience in her life, she is narrating her self through a certain period of time and space. This voicing of self in story form is perhaps the most basic form of human communication. The following self-authoring activities illustrate what constructing an autobiographical self means.

91

Activity 1: Listening and learning from stories

In listening to the help-seeker's story, the counsellor can take a stance of empathy, asking questions that encourage the help-seeker to continue and questions that *generate meaning.* The counsellor's questions should encourage the storyteller to describe and narrate from a personal point of view and not resort to abstractions and explanations. The main effort is to encourage the story teller to follow the rule, "This is my story, what I experienced, and what this story means to me."

As the counsellor listens to the help-seeker's stories, there are certain story elements that can be listened for:

1. Most importantly, What is this story conveying, what seems to be the purpose of the story?
2. Does the story make sense? Is it coherent?
3. Does there seem to something missing from this story?
4. Are there ideas that appear repeatedly in the story?
5. Who are the characters in this story? In particular, is this story a report of the narrator's own experience, or is the story being told "about" someone else?
6. What seems to be the key point in this story?
7. How does hearing this story influence your perception of the storyteller? What are you own reactions to hearing this story?
8. Does this story sound insightful for the help-seeker, or is it more a description of personal trouble, a lamentation, an accusation, or something else?

Making a map of the story can accompany the help-seeker's telling of her story. Sometimes the mapping is initiated right at the beginning of the story, or part way through. Of course, it is not essential to map, but the mapping will enable some help-seekers to tell their story with greater detail and meaning and even more insight.

Activity 2: Mapping multiple voices: Bakhtin's hotel

Mikhail Bakhtin once observed that we could think of a self as a hotel with many rooms. In each of those rooms a voice has taken up permanent residence, suggesting that as a self we have many voices. Some of these are active voices of our present self and life-space. Other voices are held in memory but are, so to speak, on the shelf in the background. For example, I am a writer, lecturer, husband, and father. I can voice myself in each of these frames of experience and do so every day. On the other hand, I was raised on a farm from my birth to fifteen years of age. From that experience, I acquired the voice of a rural person and a farmer. Those voices remain in my memory but are seldom spoken, since I live as an academic in a cosmopolitan social setting.

The "Bakhtin's hotel" self-authoring activity is as follows:

1. Explain to the help-seeker that we develop different voices as we experience new aspects of social life, getting to a point where we can voice that experience as "one who knows" about that form of life. Give several examples of this phenomenon.

2. Have the help-seeker draw a one-dimensional hotel on a piece of paper with a number of rooms. I usually suggest fifteen to thirty rooms. Then ask the help-seeker to write in and name a voice in each room. I usually do this activity along with the help-seeker. Sometimes I ask the help-seeker to indicate at approximately what age they began to speak with each voice and to write that number also in each room.

3. Once the help-seeker (and yourself if you are also doing the activity) has completed writing in the voices, then you can stimulate dialogue about the meanings of these voices for the help-seeker. Helpful questions include:

- Which voices are more important to you and why?
- Which voice(s) do you think are the most involved in your present concern? Can any of your voices help you? In what way?
- Are there voices that you wish you had, but don't?

- Which voices do you think give you the greatest strength to cope in daily living?
- Are there voices that you wish that you did not have?

The helper can initiate a dialogue and discussion with the help-seeker about how voices can help a person to understand that he or she is not just one thing. Voices and stories told are sources for developing, solving, and becoming. Voices tell stories, and stories can be listened to and rewritten. Stories are a primal form of human communication. This is the essence of self-authoring.

Counsellors and psychologists who have been trained to look for answers in behaviour and personality structure may have difficulty in understanding the concept of self-as-narrator. A paradigmatic shift in thinking is required. From the SocioDynamic perspective, it is not fruitful to look for the meaning of stories in personality structure as is sometimes done in psychodynamic work. The behaviour of individuals is motivated and guided by the meaning structures of the self.

From the self-authoring perspective, the self is not so much an entity, a biophysical structure, but more a capacity, energy, or an evolving text.[50] As Jerome Bruner[51] has written, the culturally shaped thought and language processes that guide self-narrating achieve a capacity to structure perception and memory and endow purpose to life events. "In the end, we become the autobiographic narratives by which we 'tell about our lives' "(p. 15).

Activity 3: Investigating the chapters of life
In this activity, the help-seeker is given the following explanation and suggestions:

As we go through life we have events or experiences that make our lives go in a new direction. The birth of a child, a life-threatening illness, a love affair, school graduation, a religious conversion, loss of employment, death of a loved one, and endless other life-altering experiences may befall us. We can think of our life as a book composed of chapters. Each chapter begins or ends with an experience or event that either ended a chapter in your life or began a new one.

94

1. *Draw a line and mark it off in five- or ten-year periods.*
2. *Decide how many chapters your life has. In other words, how many times have you experienced something that made your life take a different direction or have a different feeling to it? Briefly note those points of change in at the approximate time a chapter began or ended.*
3. *Once you have decided upon the chapters of your life, try to decide on a name for each chapter.*
4. *Finally, pick out the chapter that has the greatest immediate interest for you and engage in a dialogue with your counsellor or a group member (if you are in group counselling).*

As the counsellor, your role is to guide the help-seeker in the process of designing book-of-life chapters. Then help to explore the meaning of the chapters and the events that started and ended chapters. This procedure is designed to

- Develop coherent understanding of the life trajectory,
- Locate pivotal events and their meanings,
- Promote reflection on experience and values,
- Help the person to develop an evaluation of personal strengths and any needs for other capacities,
- Clarify self-identity, and
- Provide a detailed context for discussion and resolution of problems in the immediate existential situation.

The self-authoring strategy enables individuals to grasp the constructive nature of the self and what is meant by self-creation. Self-authoring does not take place in isolation from others. In one sense, it is more accurate to use the term "self co-authoring," since we always exist in the context of relationships with others. Most of the stories we create about our lives are, in fact, strongly influenced by what others say to us and the impression we wish to make on others. In any self-narrative, the relationship between the narrator and the characters in her story tells much about how and why this particular autobiographical story is created.

Activity 4: Listing and exploring the meaning of self-descriptions
This self-authoring activity has five steps: 1) listing self-features and/or capacities that the individual now possesses (the help-seeker is asked to use either single words or short phrases); 2) identifying those descriptions that indicate positive strength characteristics; 3) identifying descriptions to be revised or discarded—characteristics that the individual wishes he or she did not possess; 4) identifying descriptions not present but desired and dialogue about how one's self and capacities would be different if changes were made or new features acquired; 5) formulating activity projects in support of strengths or initiatives to construct new capacities or characteristics.

This activity begins with the counsellor suggesting that the help-seeker make a list of words or short phrases that indicate fifteen to twenty important characteristics of self. These can be either positive self-features or can describe characteristics that the person does not see favourably.

The second step is to go through the list, drawing a circle around those words that the help-seeker believes are important and positive features of self. In the third step, the help-seeker is asked to draw a line through those words that name undesirable characteristics. After identifying both positive and negative features, their consequences are discussed and explored by helper and help-seeker. Then the help-seeker is asked what he or she would like to be able to list about self and asked to write down a short list of the most important features he or she would like to have. When that is done, the helper and help-seeker discuss the possibility of acquiring each of these and how having the characteristic would influence the life and capacity of the help-seeker.

There is also discussion about the reality of the features listed and what constraints and opportunities will have to be dealt with if the help-seeker wishes actually to develop this feature or capacity. The last step of this guided participation activity is to work together to devise realistic projects that the help-seeker can initiate that are designed to develop the desired feature or capacity. Figure 4 presents listings made by a female help-seeker.

Figure 4. Words That Describe Me.

My list of words that describe me:

Tense, careful, determined, loyal, caring, resentful, worried, shy, lonely, good worker, up-to-date office skills, uncertainty in new situations, single parent, shaky relations with manager, intelligent, stressed, not very physically fit.

My strengths (underlined):

Tense, <u>careful</u>, <u>determined</u>, <u>loyal</u>, <u>caring</u>, resentful, worried, shy, lonely, <u>good worker</u>, <u>up-to-date office skills</u>, uncertainty in new situations, <u>single parent</u>, shaky relations with manager, <u>intelligent</u>, stressed, not very physically fit.

What I'd most like to get rid of (strike through):

Tense, careful, determined, loyal, caring, ~~resentful~~, worried, shy, ~~lonely~~, good worker, up-to-date office skills, uncertainty in new situations, single parent, ~~shaky relations with manager~~, intelligent, stressed, ~~not very physically fit~~.

Characteristics that I wish I had:

[Belonging], [ability to talk with my superior without getting resentful], [good physical condition].

Personal activity projects that my counsellor and I have discussed and created for me to try out:

The following text summarizes what the help-seeker had to say about her personal projects. She had come to counselling for help in reducing some tension and conflict at her workplace.

I feel that two projects are enough for me to work on at the present time, so I chose the most important issues for me: physical fitness and better relations with my manager. My counsellor and I worked out the two projects that made sense to me and to which I feel that I can make a firm commitment.

97

Project 1. *I will make an appointment with my doctor for a general physical examination and talk to him about my need for more exercise. I live close enough to work that I can walk to work in about 45 minutes. I have agreed with my counsellor that I can try walking to work and taking the bus home or taking the bus to work and then walking home, whichever works out best for me on a day-to-day basis. I have done this in the past a couple of times, and I actually enjoyed the walk. I am a pretty determined person, so I think I could stick to this and it would be a form of regular exercise for me.*

Project 2. *I have worked in this office for about two years now. A number of times, I have tried to negotiate some conditions with my manager. We don't seem to communicate very well. I get flustered and later I feel really resentful. Probably it's partly my fault and partly hers. Anyway, I would like to do something about it, since otherwise my job goes quite well.*

My counsellor and I agreed on a two-part project for me to do. First, I will sit down at my computer and type out a letter (not to be mailed) in which I carefully describe the working condition(s) I would like to change, and then I will write several sentences that I think would clearly and politely make my requests. After that I will write a short scenario on how I think the conversation will go. Then I will bring the letter back to my counsellor, and we will go over it together and maybe even role-play the conversation, with my counsellor acting as the manager.

The second part of my activity project is to have a discussion with a colleague in the office about my difficulty in talking with the manager and see if she has any good ideas for me. She and I have become trusted friends; she has worked there quite a while and seems to have no trouble with the manager at all. If she is willing to talk with me about it, she might be able to suggest what I need to do differently or how I need to approach my manager. I plan to talk with her and write the letter. After I have finished both, I will make another appointment with my counsellor to discuss the results of my project work and how I can benefit by it.

Activity 5: Life-space co-investigation as a source of strength and capacity building.

This counselling activity brings two SocioDynamic concepts into play with each other: the *autobiographical self* and the *life-space.* The autobiographical self is that self we create through the stories we tell to others, the inner dialogues we have with ourselves, the conversations we have about who and what we are, and the personal documents (diaries, logs, letters, and other personal writings) about ourselves and our experiences in life.

The autobiographical self is created primarily through our symbolic interactions with others. It is continuously evolving and is a complex configuration of interacting semantic meaning systems. Although it "resides" in the brain and nervous system, it is primarily constituted and maintained through our communication with others and with the world around us. We author our self and co-author it with those around us with whom we have communication.

The life-space refers to all those forces, both inside and outside ourselves, that influence us at any moment. We know our life-space through our ideas and perceptions of it, the meanings it has for us, and our activities and interactions with others and the material world that surrounds us.

The life-space is made up of experience, meanings, objects of perception, activities in social life, and the solitude of being alone. The following diagram shows the five life-space sectors and their interconnections: world view, health, work and education, relationships, and play.

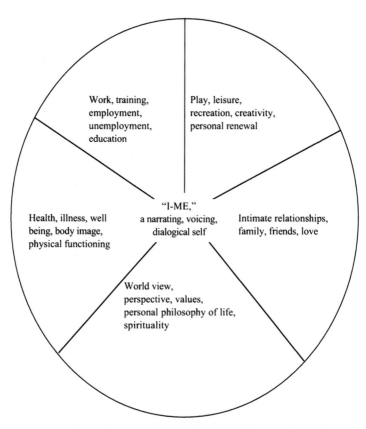

Figure 5. Life-Space Sectors.

Work, training, employment, unemployment, education

Play, leisure, recreation, creativity, personal renewal

Health, illness, well being, body image, physical functioning

"I-ME," a narrating, voicing, dialogical self

Intimate relationships, family, friends, love

World view, perspective, values, personal philosophy of life, spirituality

These life-space sectors make up most of the meaning sources in an individual's life-space. While a particular concern of the help-seeker may be located primarily in one of the sectors, there usually will be interconnections with other sectors. For example, if a person becomes unemployed, this may also be accompanied by increased stress and even illness. The person's relationships may be affected, and certainly his or her perspective will be influenced.

The life-space helps to place any problem or concern in the context of the person's whole life. A person is a complex, whole system. The functioning of any subsystem will have repercussions throughout the total system. Therefore, the SocioDynamic perspective views counselling from a *holistic* stance. Most of the time, it is wise for the counsellor to perceive a help-seeker as a person-in-context and not single out a discrete aspect of the individual or remove the problem or person from his or her everyday functional contexts.

While keeping the whole person-in-context in mind, it also is important to focus on the particulars of the problem for which the person seeks help. It is important to ask the help-seeker *meaning-generating* questions, whether attention is on a particular aspect of a life-space sector, on the whole sector, or even on the interconnections between sectors and the whole life-space. For example, some useful questions to ask are (a map can be developed using the answers to these questions):

- Who are the other people involved in this concern in addition to yourself?
- In what way are they involved, from your perspective?
- What are you thinking and/or doing in relation to the problem at the moment?
- What do you think are the main effects this concern is having on your life on a day-to-day basis?
- How do you think your life would change if this problem did not exist?
- From your point of view, what is stopping you from finding a way to resolve this difficulty? How are you being blocked in any attempts you make to find a solution that is workable?
- If you suddenly had the power to do so, what would be the main thing you would change to make your situation better?
- What do you know how to do that might help you make this situation better? Do you think that there is something you could learn to do that would give you the necessary strength to overcome this difficulty?
- Who else might be able to help you?

- If someone else had the problem you are describing, and their situation was exactly like yours, and you were standing on the outside looking in on their predicament, what would you tell them that might help them find a solution? Imagine that you were from some other world and that you could see the difficulty clearly and were not affected by it yourself. What would you say to that person?

By guiding a person in the making of a life-space map, or some portion of it, and by asking questions that help bring out meanings and coordinate how the person is thinking about his or her difficulty and reactions to it, a helper often can assist the person to discover personal resources of which he or she has been unaware. This is also a way to identify capacities needed for achieving a solution. This method helps both counsellor and help-seeker to establish links between the focal problem and the surrounding context(s). The most important tools used in this activity are guided participation, life-space mapping, meaning-generating questions, and co-investigation. The counsellor guides the process, and the help-seeker provides the content.

The Way of the "Bricoleur"

Many professional counsellors have been trained to believe that it is very important to have a validated, formalized intervention to apply to particular problems. From a SocioDynamic perspective, such an intervention may be useful occasionally, but more typically, there is no already existing intervention that can be applied like a formula.

Instead, counsellors are like the *bricoleur* of Lévi-Strauss[52]—a kind of jack-of-all-trades on the professional level. Bricoleurs *create* solutions to problems; they do not apply preconceived interventions. They use the material-at-hand, including various ideas and new assemblages of information and experience, together with careful observation of the existential situation of the help-seeker, and they follow the rule of the "best guess." Counsellors-as-bricoleurs know that they are not working with predictability and certainties. They cobble together possible alternatives, whatever resources are available, and the capacities of the help-seeker and depend on dialogue, cultural awareness, intuition, stories, and shared observations and reflections. For the bricoleur, counselling is an art. Invention is not merely the child of necessity; it is a *demand* of the art of helping.

When the counsellor-as-bricoleur faces a help-seeker, she knows that the materials at hand include the help-seeker's life experience and knowledge, her own life experience and knowledge, and the constraints and opportunities of the help-seeker's existential situation. Using her intelligence, imagination, perception, and memory combined with those same elements on the part of the help-seeker, she guides the process of cobbling together the most sensible solution that they can invent. The operating rule of the bricoleur is "Let's put our heads together and see what we can come up with."

Empathic Attunement

There is sound research evidence that empathic listening enables a help-seeker to articulate his or her life experience and can be considered a helpful strategy in itself. For example, Greenberg and Watson[53] found that empathic counselling was equally effective compared both with an active counselling process using "strong" techniques and with cognitive therapy. How can this be?

If the counsellor views help-seekers as active, creative persons capable of thinking and exploring, and not as passive, helpless or sick, then a very different perspective emerges on how a help-seeker can benefit from empathic listening. The main benefits are that empathic listening clarifies and deepens the help-seeker's expressions of life experience, leading to new insights and a clearer recognition of both strengths and constraints, and that the help-seeker experiences the relationship with the helper as one of *being-with*. The helper as a cooperative partner in personal problem solving is a profoundly supportive condition.

When a help-seeker is in the presence of a helper who is empathically attuned, the help-seeker feels safe and inspired to think, imagine, feel, and act with more *self-direction* than when the counsellor is prescribing and intervening. Providing another with the experience of being truly understood without criticism is to provide one of the most fundamental conditions of learning. When a person is listened to in an empathic, unconditional manner, she has better access to her memories and is able to express feelings such as shame, guilt, and anxiety without the fear of not being taken seriously.

Finally, empathy supports the help-seeker's capacity to articulate and reflect on his experience of the problem and the relevant elements of his life-space. The help-seeker is supported in using his or her *intuitive* understanding and reaction to the troubling situation. When help-seekers express their existential situation as they perceive it, including constraints and possibilities, and in terms of their own ideas and feelings, they are, as Bohart and Tallman[54] put it, expressing *ecological wisdom*. While ecological wisdom may need altering or may be at odds with the counsellor's perceptions, at any given moment it represents the best interpretation of the life-space that a help-seeker has to offer. The counsellor should respect it and take it seriously; that is, it should receive empathic listening.

Group Counselling and Other Social Supports
From a SocioDynamic perspective, most learning takes place through interpersonal interaction and communication. Another way of saying this is that learning is mediated through social relations. I will briefly describe group counselling and guided participation/ mentoring/net-working as social relations strategies to be used to promote learning and capacity building.

Group counselling
SocioDynamic group counselling methods are organized around three constructivist learning principles:

1. Group counselling can provide learning conditions for members to build their capacities and revise their perspectives.
2. Group counselling should use activity based learning.

3. People learn best when they receive encouragement and constructive support, both of which are provided by well-conducted groups.

In SocioDynamic group work, the counsellor functions as guide to the group process. It is the responsibility of the counsellor to

- See that group members are provided supportive "warming-up" discussion and introduction.
- Assume responsibility for organizing the activity in a way that is emotionally safe for participants. Participants should be "ready" for any activity, especially those that include self-disclosure.
- Adapt the learning activity to the level of capacity, learning needs, and knowledge of the participants so they can be expected to experience some success in doing the activity.
- Arrange a meeting environment that is free from distraction and that provides reasonable privacy.
- Recognize that group members have differing needs and capacities and operate at different levels in terms of speed and motivation.
- Protect listening and reinforce the idea that helping others is valued and that interfering with the learning of others or the process is not valued.
- Model communication, especially dialogical communication.
- Introduce activities to group members that are intended to increase capacity, strengthen self identity and esteem, provide useful knowledge and data, and provide time for reflection on learning experience and dialogue with other members and the counsellor about learning experiences and possible applications to everyday life.

An example of SocioDynamic group counselling is a group meeting of eight refugee women from Somalia, Bosnia, Afghanistan, and Iraq. Together they met with the group counsellor for a period of about two hours. All spoke English, from very limited to fairly fluent. After some warming-up discussion and sharing of personal information, the counsellor introduced the group activity of mapping (drawing) the homes they had lived in before becoming refugees.

They were given paper and different coloured pencils and shown maps made in an earlier group by a Kenyan and a Bosnian. The counsellor emphasized that they should feel free to use their imagination and not worry about their drawing ability. What was stressed as important was to include details and illustration of living functions and where different members of the family lived and slept. The counsellor joined in the activity.

The counsellor stated that after about half an hour, they would be able to show each other their work, ask and answer questions, and talk together about where they lived in their country of origin, what kind of abode they now lived in, and the problems they and members of their families were experiencing in making the transition. Following the mapping period, the group participants and counsellor engaged in a lively show-and-tell discussion for nearly an hour.

Some of the topics discussed by group members included:

- The difficulties of getting their children to and from school and the different ways the schools were run compared with their own school experience.
- Problems of getting food that they were culturally accustomed to eating.
- Both relief and sadness about being away from their original dwellings.
- Children's behaviours changing in the new context.
- Resentment about being pressured to prepare for employment when they primarily wanted to be at home caring for their children.

The discussion was lively, there was quite a lot of laughing as the women shared their experiences and needs with each other, and several new friendships were initiated. The women were helped to articulate their life experience, share problems, and listen to examples of what others had done in similar circumstances.

There are several approaches to arranging groups so that the participants have learning and dialogue opportunities.

1. Use *activity-based dialogue*. As in the example above, in which participants engage in mapping, use a common activity as a base from which to begin dialogue and learn different ways of cultural-coping,

2. Use *text-based dialogue*. Have members of a group read some text—document, letter, for example—and then initiate dialogue from the text material encouraging participants to express personal experiences and reactions triggered by reading the text.

3. Use *writing-based dialogue*. Have participants write a short piece regarding a topic or experience that is potentially meaningful to all. Possible topics include: The kind of job that I am best at. What I hope to get out of my training. What I would like to change about my working life. The job I have always dreamed about but have never had. My reaction to the new employment policy. Things that keep me from being more healthy.

4. Use *object- or image-based dialogue*. Show pictures, slides, videos, films, or objects to a group and ask them to jot down their main reactions to what they have seen. Then initiate dialogue and encourage articulation of personal experience in relation to what has been viewed. With some groups, it may be necessary to go directly to the dialogue rather than writing.

Constructivist learning in groups is based on participants' active participation in problem solving and critical thinking regarding a learning activity that they find relevant and engaging. They are "constructing" their own knowledge by testing ideas and approaches based on their prior knowledge and experience, applying these to a new situation, and integrating the new knowledge gained with pre-existing constructs.

Guided participation/mentoring/networking

Guided participation, a term employed by Rogoff,[55] refers to the mutual involvement of individuals and their social partners as they communicate and coordinate structured, collective socio-cultural activity. For example, when two people engage in an activity together, they observe each other's actions and speech, and they coordinate their joint activities for some common purpose. Their relation need not be symmetrical. In the case of apprenticeship, an individual who is learning a skill will learn actively from a more experienced individual by observing, imitating, and actively appropriating skills and knowledge from the more experienced.

Interpersonal communication and coordination are central ideas in the notion of guided participation. Communication and coordination occur as persons participate in shared endeavours. The shared activity is not random, but has a direction or purpose. As partners or members of a group direct their activities toward explicit, implicit, or emerging goals, they may or may not be able to articulate their goals clearly. The participants' involvement is motivated by some purpose, and their actions are deliberate. The purpose of the activity may be task-oriented, such as finding and learning practical ways to apply for employment. Or the purpose may be more social—to spend time enjoyably together or to provide mutual support in the face of trying circumstances.

Mentoring is a good example of guided participation. Mentoring is a social relation in which one individual tries to actively learn from another more experienced (model) thorough the processes of observation and communication (dialogue) and by mutually carrying out activities. The more experienced partner does not necessarily directly instruct the other, but instead discusses, shows by example, and engages in common activities.

A mentoring relationship is best when there is a common desire to participate in the mentoring arrangement and the mentor is generally recognized as having very good skill and judgement in the activities or role in which the less-experienced partner is wishing to become more skilful.

Conditions of trust and interpersonal compatibility are very important in mentoring. An example of a mentoring project is the role-model project in a First Nations community in northern British Columbia. The tribal counsellors have compiled a list of First Nations adults who are respected in the community and who are successful in their work. The counsellors arrange to match up mentors and protegés. A young and inexperienced individual who is interested in learning how to be a successful art shop salesperson will be introduced to an art shop owner who has an interest in mentoring a protegé. The arrangement must be mutually agreed upon and depends very much on the degree of interest on the part of both partners to participate in a mutual, trustworthy, learning-thorough-participation relationship. Financial stipends for the novices vary and may be provided through a work scholarship program.

Related to mentoring but less coordinated is membership in networks. Networks have several important features. Generally, they are either primarily informational or socially supportive. They may be face-to-face or at a distance (for example an Internet group organized around a common interest, such as a health issue or employment). A useful distinction to make about networks is that they may be characterized by either weak or strong ties. Some Internet networks start out as primarily informational and evolve into stronger ties providing personal support for network members. Examples include *SeniorNet* for elderly people and *Systers*, a network for female computer scientists.

In as much as workplaces, families, and institutions depend more and more on networking, even to the point that some[56] refer to contemporary society as the *network society,* it is a good idea for counsellors to assist help-seekers to learn how to participate actively in networks.

Chapter 4: A SocioDynamic Counselling Practice Scenario

In this chapter I present a prototypical case illustrating various features of SocioDynamic counselling. This is the story of a real counselling case. However, some portions have been fictionalized for purposes of confidentiality and to provide a clear description of the ideas and practices that are used in the SocioDynamic method. Not all principles that guide SocioDynamic counselling are included, but many of the important ideas are illustrated.

In this scenario the counsellor (C) is myself. The help-seeker is a seventeen-year-old male whose name is Mark (M). He is attending secondary school intermittently and is doing barely passing work in his studies. He was referred to me along with the following information:

His parents are worried that he does not seem motivated to succeed in school and has no plans for his future. Moreover, he refuses to discuss these matters with them. He recently had a counselling session with the school counsellor. The counsellor reported that their meeting was not successful because the help-seeker would not talk with him and did not seem to show any interest in either school or counselling.

Mark had also been referred to a private psychologist who reported that he could not establish any communication with the help-seeker and therefore would not see him again. His report described the help-seeker as resistant, antagonistic, and possibly depressed.

I received a telephone call from Mark. He said that he had agreed with his parents and his school advisor that he would come to me for counselling. I asked him what he wanted to see me about. He replied that partly it was just to get his parents "off his back." He also said that he would like to talk things over with someone who was not connected to school or his family. I gave him directions to my study, and we made an appointment for an hour-long meeting on the following Wednesday morning. In the following case description, I will insert the SocioDynamic principles that guided me in italic type where it is appropriate to do so.

First Counselling Session

Meeting others where they are. As I thought about what I had been told about Mark and his apparent refusal to talk to his parents or other helpers, I imagined that his refusal might have been because others wanted him to talk about what *they* thought was important. Bringing up topics like school studies, his future, his lack of interest in school may have been what others wanted to talk about but not what he wanted to discuss.

A very important idea in SocioDynamic counselling is the concept of *common ground*. If Mark and I are to build some common ground to stand on, then I should try to begin our discussion with something that he is interested in discussing and that has personal meaning to him. In other words, I should try to begin discussion on some topic that has meaning for him in his present life-space. I should not be guided by what I expect or want him to discuss. I wish to be able to enter into his life-space by opening up for discussion some topic from his present life that has meaning for him. I wish to gain some understanding of how and why he is living his life as he is at the present time. I realize also that he is seventeen and I am seventy, so there is a potentially large generational gap between us.

On Wednesday, there is a knock at my front door. I open it and Mark is standing there. He is a slightly built person. We shake hands and I lead the way to my study. I tell him that I am pleased that he decided to see me. I also say that we will have an hour to talk things over. He takes a seat on a couch, and I sit on my computer chair.

We exchange a few "social approach" comments. I try to present a *human face* to Mark. By that I mean that I do not wish to convey an attitude of being superior, official, an advice-giver, or a person who gives the impression of "knowing more or what is best." Even though we are different in age and experience, I wish to meet him as *one human being meeting another human being.* I wish to be seen as a person who is attentive, interested, open to discuss whatever is relevant to Mark, *respectful*, and reflective. I want my face to convey respect and spontaneity and reveal my own attitudes of seriousness and playfulness.

To show a human face does not mean denying differences in experience and social position; it does mean displaying respect for the other as a unique and valuable person who has important life experiences to articulate and discuss. It also means conveying an attitude of open-mindedness to alternative views and a willingness to establish a cooperative, communicative relationship. This sets the stage for *joint action* and makes it possible for both persons to make important contributions to the counselling dialogue. Displaying a human face means to recognize that both helper and help-seeker are members of a common humanity, which should not be erased by adherence to professional or status roles.

Of course, a counsellor must observe appropriate boundaries and maintain an ethical stance between self and other, but these responsibilities do not require taking on the persona of a distanced, objective official. From a SocioDynamic point of view, the helper should *maintain an objective attitude toward self while remaining subjective (open-minded) toward others*. To maintain objectivity toward self means to remain aware of one's own reactions toward the other, to be alert to possible biases and premature judgements, and to remain aware of one's own communication.

I ask Mark if he came by bus. He replies that he borrowed his mother's car. He has a friend living in my neighbourhood so he had no difficulty finding my house. He comments, "You sure have a lot of books," and I reply, "Yes, that is how I make my living—studying and writing." He asks me if I have actually read all of these books. I reply that I have read most of them, but that sometimes I get a book that seems like it would be interesting and then I find it not so interesting, so I just put it aside. He laughs and says, "I sure know how that is, especially the books I am supposed to read in school." This dialogue reveals we have begun to establish a small island of *common ground*.

Is the help-seeker *ready* for counselling? *Readiness* is an important concept in SocioDynamic counselling. A person will only

113

engage in an activity, or learn about something, if he is ready to do so. The concept of readiness replaces the concept of "resistance." Resistance implies that the other regards you as an opponent or enemy. Most of the time, what the other is experiencing is lack of readiness—he is not sure what is going to happen or does not know whether or not to proceed. The counsellor's first task may be to take steps to bring the help-seeker into a state of readiness. Often this can be accomplished by briefly discussing what happens in counselling or finding some common ground before proceeding on to problem solving.

I ask Mark if he has had counselling before, and he says, "Yes, but it didn't help me—the counsellor mostly asked me about my classes in school." I explain to him that he and I both had some work to do for counselling to be helpful, that I would do the best I can to listen carefully to what he wants to talk about and that he has the job of telling me something about how his life is going. I say, "We are in this together—together maybe we can figure something out for you."

Mark has a somewhat sceptical look on his face and says, "Are you going to tell me what to do?" I say, "No, I am not going to tell you what to do. I may have some ideas to share with you, but in the end what you decide about will be up to you." I then tell him, "Mark, you and I don't know anything at all about each other. Maybe it would be helpful if we had an idea about how we spend our days. If you can start, it would be very useful to me to know what it is that you do that you find quite interesting to do. What is it that 'turns you on' these days?" Mark looks at me with a quizzical smile on his face and says, "Are you serious?" I reply, "Yes, I would like to hear about something that you do—an activity— that means a lot to you." He hesitates for a moment and then says, "OK, what I like doing best is skateboarding."

"Mark," I say, "I know very little about skateboarding. So fill me in on what it is about skateboarding that is so interesting to you." *The door to Mark's life-space opens* as he begins to tell *the story of one his deeply embedded life interests.* A good counselling session is more a narration of relevant stories than an "interview." "Deeply embedded life interests" are those interests in life about which a person feels strongly and that he or she feels a desire to do or experience whenever possible.

For almost an hour, Mark tells me the story of himself and skateboarding. I am almost completely ignorant about this topic. An hour later, I know a lot about the technical aspects of skateboards, where in the city skateboarding is permitted and where not, skateboard contests and rules, where skateboard equipment is sold, and many of Mark's personal experiences with skateboarding and his friends. This is a very good example of the constructivist principle of *taking the position of "not-knowing" and letting the help-seeker teach you about his life.*

As Mark tells me about the importance of skateboarding in his life, I listen and ask him a few *meaning-generating questions,* such as:

What is your experience like when you are in a skateboard contest?

What does skateboarding add to your life?

Do you think skateboarding teaches you anything about yourself?

If, for some reason, you were not able to skateboard anymore, what would that mean to you?

How does skateboarding fit in with the other things you do every day?

For the most part, I listen quietly to him talk, and from time to time I use *empathic reiteration* to demonstrate what I have understood him to say. An important principle of SocioDynamic counselling is that the helper should validate the help-seeker's descriptions of his or her life experience and the meaning of that experience for the help-seeker. Validation of the other's experience is accomplished by remaining respectful of what is being said and using both meaning-generating questions and reiteration to confirm that understanding has occurred. I encourage Mark to describe his experiences of skateboarding and to give me concrete examples so that I can understand better what he is telling me.

115

Mark then narrates several humorous experiences he has had as a skateboarder, and we laugh together. For the better part of an hour I am *attentive, interested, respectful, and actively engaged* in the conversation as a dialogical listener.

At the end of our discussion about skateboarding, I ask him, "How do you experience going to school?" He replies, "I don't like it. I know that I need to finish secondary school and maybe go on to university, but right now I am just not interested. Everyone is telling me how much potential I have. I know that already. I'd like to do something else for a while until I am ready to get serious about school."

Near the end of the hour, I say to Mark, "We have used up our time for today. We haven't got to what you came to see me about but we have got a start. Do you want to come back again?" He says, "Sure, it's been good to talk with you."

Encouraging reflection on the counselling process, at the end of the hour, I say to Mark, "Before we stop, I'd like to trade comments with you about our counselling discussion today. Maybe you can say something about how you think it went for you and then I will do the same."

M: *When I came here today, I wasn't sure there was much point in it. Mostly when I have talked to the counsellor at school or my parents or the psychologist, they have told me that I should think seriously about my future and what I am going to do after I graduate and how important it is to get better grades. I thought you might talk to me the same way.*

I was really surprised that you seemed interested in my skateboarding. Mostly what I've heard from other people is that skateboards are a waste of my time and money and that it is dangerous for me or a nuisance for other people. I really enjoyed talking to you.

He laughs and says, *I guess that is because I did most of the talking. I also thought it was neat when you told me that playing sports had been a very important thing for you when you were my age. I hadn't thought of you as someone who had ever played football.*

116

I then tell Mark several of my impressions of our counselling conversation.

C: *Mark, I was impressed by* your knowledge *of skateboarding and how you have gained some insight into yourself and your own needs through your experience as a skateboarder. I also think that you and I have got a feel for each other so that we can talk easily about what you would like to do in your life, whatever that is.*

I try to end every counselling session with an exchange of comments on our time together. This allows both of us to *self-observe* and make some statement about the counselling process or report on our own experience during the counselling conversation. The capacity for *self-observation (reflection)* is quite important in problem solving and in constructing beneficial relationships. For my part, I usually try to highlight some strength or insight the help-seeker has described during the conversation and add my own reaction to what I have observed. In this way, I add a small contribution in the direction of *validating the self or the experience of the help-seeker.*

As he gets up to leave, I say to Mark, "We can meet the same time next week. When you come, I would like to hear about something else in your life that is interesting to you. You have told me a whole lot about skateboarding, so let's take up something else." He laughs and says, "OK." We shake hands and he leaves.

Second Counselling Session

The following Wednesday, Mark arrives and we go down to my study. We exchange a few pleasantries, and then I *suggest that we explore another aspect of his life-space of his own choosing* by asking, "So what is on your mind that we have not talked about yet?" The purpose of the conversation is to assist Mark to articulate what is meaningful to him in his own life-space at the moment. Does he have any *newly emerging life interests*? By directing attention to the immediate, constructive present, a starting point can be built to explore some alternatives from which he

117

can choose to move forward. In other words, possible futures are always initiated from a good grasp of the present. Mark and I are *co-investigating and thinking together* about activities, meanings, and interests in his life-space. This may reveal possible futures.

M: *I had a very interesting conversation with a girl at school last week.*

C: *What did the two of you talk about?*

M: *Well, she had been in Israel last year, living on a kibbutz. I didn't even know what a Kibbutz was until I talked with her.*

C: *What was it that you found so interesting?*

M: *Oh lots of things, the work she did, her friends, the culture, travelling, etc. I thought to myself, "Boy, would I like to do something like that."*

C: *So, you could see yourself travelling to Israel and having some experiences like the ones your friend told you about.*

M: *Absolutely. But I don't know. What would I have to do to go there anyway?*

Mark is beginning to *imagine a possible future* for himself. From the SocioDynamic perspective, a future is created in three phases. First, an individual must be able to *imagine* a possible future. Next, the individual must *desire* (perceive the possible future as personally meaningful). Third, the individual must act to realize the future. A future that materializes out of the resources of the individual is much more likely to be constructed than a future that is suggested by another person.

At this point, I tell Mark that like him, I don't know very much about a kibbutz. However, we can use my computer to look for some current, relevant information. *A task of the helper is to assist the help-seeker to access meaningful data or information that meets a genuine need of the help-seeker.* He and I pull chairs up to the computer screen, and sitting side-by-side, we search the Internet for Israel and kibbutz Web sites. *SocioDynamic counselling is based on the assumption that it is better to work together as partners whenever possible.* This process has at least two virtues:

1. It reinforces a good working relationship.
2. It allows for the intelligence of both helper and help-seeker to be active in the problem solving.

Shortly, we find a highly informative Web site on the various kibbutzim that can be visited in Israel. Together we read about the character of each kibbutz—the economy, location, climate, geography, population, and so on. Mark and I, together with the computer, have a kind of three-way conversation that is relevant and meaningful to both Mark and myself. We point out various things of interest to each other. There is a kind of *learning through guided participation*, where Mark and I are guiding each other as we investigate new territory in his life-space (and mine as well). I have good ideas about what to look for on the Internet, and Mark is more skilful and swift in using the computer keyboard than I am. Together we make a very competent research team. The computer guides both of us with presentation of relevant data.

> M: *I sure would like to go to Israel and stay for a while on a kibbutz. Do you think I could do that?*
> C: *I can't think of any reason why you could not do that if you really want to and are willing to take the necessary steps. We could make a plan for you. Would you like to do that?*
> M: *Sure.*
> C: *We can make a map or drawing of your situation that can serve as a plan to guide you if you are serious about preparing to go to a kibbutz, OK?*
> Mark begins to put down his ideas on a piece of paper and then says,
> M: *One of the pages we looked at in the computer gave a list of what is needed for a person who wants to go to live on a kibbutz. We can use that to see what steps I need to take.* (I print a hard copy).

On a sheet of paper, Mark and I, working together, make a drawing that represents his current life-space. Together we try to think of all the important tasks and concerns that are related to a decision on his part to go to Israel. An important practice in SocioDynamic counselling is the use of *visualization and mapping* to develop understanding of complex life situations, especially aspects of one's life-space. *Mapping is a cooperative activity*, with the helper contributing the structure and the help-seeker contributing the content. *Mapping and dialogue go hand in hand.* On the following page is a simulated map taken from the hand-drawn map that Mark made. I ask him questions, such as, "Who are the people who are in some way involved in a decision you might make to go to Israel?" and, "What are the steps you will have to take in order to get ready to go?" He then puts the answers on the paper to make a planning map as follows (see Figure 6):

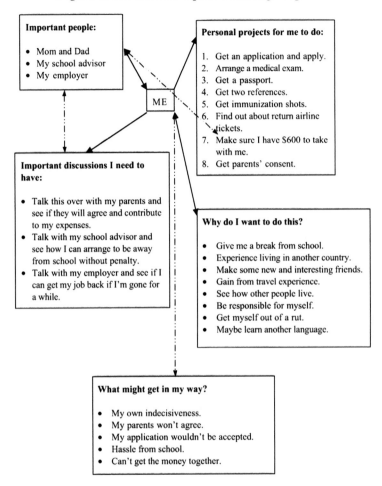

Figure 6. Mark's Life-Space Planning Map.

Important people:

- Mom and Dad
- My school advisor
- My employer

ME

Personal projects for me to do:

1. Get an application and apply.
2. Arrange a medical exam.
3. Get a passport.
4. Get two references.
5. Get immunization shots.
6. Find out about return airline tickets.
7. Make sure I have $600 to take with me.
8. Get parents' consent.

Important discussions I need to have:

- Talk this over with my parents and see if they will agree and contribute to my expenses.
- Talk with my school advisor and see how I can arrange to be away from school without penalty.
- Talk with my employer and see if I can get my job back if I'm gone for a while.

Why do I want to do this?

- Give me a break from school.
- Experience living in another country.
- Make some new and interesting friends.
- Gain from travel experience.
- See how other people live.
- Be responsible for myself.
- Get myself out of a rut.
- Maybe learn another language.

What might get in my way?

- My own indecisiveness.
- My parents won't agree.
- My application wouldn't be accepted.
- Hassle from school.
- Can't get the money together.

When Mark and I complete his map, we discuss what the various parts of it mean to him. We also talk about whether or not he feels that he can do the personal projects on his own. He says that he thinks he can. He has never purchased airline tickets and he does not know where to apply for a passport. We find the telephone number of the office to which he can apply for a passport. He says that he wants to discuss this plan with his parents and see if they would help him with finances. He has some money of his own, but probably not enough to pay all of the costs.

He takes the map with the list of personal projects and says that he wants to come back in two weeks to talk over his decision and what he has done, if his decision is to go to Israel. Again, we trade comments about today's counselling. He says that the map would help him discuss his idea with his parents and maybe even his school advisor. I tell him that today has been a good discussion for me too, since I have learned a lot about going to live on a kibbutz that I had not known before. I also tell him that I am quite impressed with the way he seemed to take responsibility for investigating the necessary arrangements. Then we shake hands and he leaves. *The counsellor leaves the decision making up to the help-seeker and provides a supportive atmosphere. Again the trading of feedback at the end of the session builds and confirms the working relationship and provides encouragement.*

Third Counselling Session

Mark arrives at my home two weeks later. He seems in very good spirits. We go to my study and he immediately says, "Guess what? I have decided to go." Then for the next thirty minutes he tells me what he has done since we met last. His story is as follows:

Well, I went right home after our last meeting. I sat down and figured out what I would say to my parents and school advisor. I also checked on how much money I have in my savings account. Then I called the office in New York and asked for an application to be sent to me. I called our family doctor and made an appointment for a check-up and to get the shots I need.

After supper, I said to my parents what I had talked with you about. At first they were really surprised, since I had not said anything to them before. But they came around and they both finally said that it seemed like a good idea to them. I have the $600 that I need to have in my pocket when I get there, but not enough to pay for tickets. My *mom said that she would give me the money I needed and that if I wanted her to, she would go to the ticket office with me to talk about the different possibilities for getting flights from Canada to Tel Aviv. Actually, they seem kind of pleased with my plan.*

I spoke to my school advisor and she said that it would not be a problem for me to leave if I finished this term first. The school would see it as a type of study-visit and I could even get some school credit for it.

I got the application last Monday. I filled it out, got my parents to write a consent note, and I have sent it back to the office in New York. I hope they approve. In the meantime, our church minister said he would write a letter of reference for me. He did that and the letter went with my application.

I say that I am amazed at how many of his personal projects he has initiated or completed. Mark says he is surprised at himself, since he had not been very interested in much except being with his friends and skateboarding for quite a while.

We then have the following conversation:

C: *What are the main things you are concerned about with regard to your decision?*
M: *Mostly, will I get accepted? Also, I have never traveled overseas before, and that is kind of scary. I don't know how I can take my skateboard either.*
C: *Maybe it would help to talk to the girl who talked to you about the kibbutz—she might have some ideas about your skateboard ... are they used at kibbutzim and did she notice anyone bringing one there? I have travelled a lot and I have ideas about what makes travelling overseas easier—would you like to hear my ideas?*
M: *Sure, I've got a lot to learn.*

We then had a discussion about how to choose clothing that travels well and needs no special care. And we talked about taking only what is absolutely necessary and adapting one's belongings to the type of climate one will be living in. This is a good example of building *common ground.*

At the end of the hour, we exchange comments on the counselling discussion and Mark says that he is very satisfied with our time together and does not know if he needs to meet with me again. He says that his mind is clearly made up that he is going, if accepted. He knows what he has to do to finish being ready to go. We agree that if he is not accepted, or if some other reason comes up and more counselling seems helpful, he will call me and we could have another meeting. We shake hands and he leaves.

Follow-Up and Comment

About a month later, I received a telephone call from Mark telling me that he was leaving for Israel in two weeks. He said that he would get in touch with me when he got back. Some months later, I had word from him that he had had a successful trip. He had arrived at one kibbutz, but after several weeks there, he had made some friends from Switzerland and Egypt and they had decided to move to another kibbutz. When their stay was up, they took a trip to Cairo and then to Zurich.

He came home by way of London, making a short stay there to visit with relatives. He was now back at home, at work again, and on much better footing with his parents. He was not planning to go back to secondary school. Instead he intended to enroll in courses at the college where he could complete the courses needed for graduation from high school. He told me that our counselling had started him on a new road in life. He was now interested in completing his education, and his new friends would be coming to Canada to visit him in the summer.

This counselling scenario outlines several significant principles of SocioDynamic counselling. Overall, it demonstrates what it means to enter into, and co-investigate the *life-space* of another person, and to work in the *constructive present*. Working in the constructive present implies that the counsellor and help-seeker try to determine what is going on at the present time in the help-seeker's existential context that is influencing the point of concern. The past and the future may be entertained but only from the perspective of their apparent influence on what is happening now. The constructive present is examined descriptively in terms of how the individual is actually experiencing it and not from the perspective of a theory or hypothesis. Certainly, our present existence is sometimes defined strongly by memories or by what we imagine. However, from the SocioDynamic perspective, it is extremely important to grasp that the past and future can only be accessed through the present.

Once a person has a reasonable understanding of his or her present existential situation, then the possibility of imagining, desiring, and acting to form more desirable futures is much more feasible. If you cannot grasp your present, you can hardly form a future. For the most part, we construct our lives out of the available materials and opportunities in the constructive present.

Some of the other principles of the SocioDynamic perspective that this counselling scenario implies are as follows:

First, it emphasizes the importance of *starting where the help-seeker is* and not starting according to the counsellor's agenda.

Second, it indicates the benefit of showing a *human face* to the help-seeker.

Third, it illustrates the value of *dialogical communication and mapping.*

Fourth, the counsellor and help-seeker engaged in *intelligent conversation,* since they were able to use dialogue, take a mindful problem-solving attitude, and comment on their own communication.

Fifth, it shows the need to maintain openness to the *multiple realities* that confront an individual. Mark had one perception of his existential situation, his parents another, and his school advisor yet another. The counsellor must guard against adopting a preset perspective on what a person should decide, or do. Instead, the counsellor's task is to assist the help-seeker to explore various realities (alternatives) and to adopt one that is *feasible and has personal meaning* for the help-seeker.

Sixth, this scenario supports the idea that counselling is both a *meaning-making process and a life-planning process.* The

125

counsellor's contribution lies in asking meaning-generating questions, using dialogical listening, clarifying, supporting, and guiding the mapping process.

Seventh, this description of counselling very clearly points out the *cooperative, co-constructing, co-investigating, co-thinking* nature of SocioDynamic counselling relationships and process. Both counsellor and help-seeker are able to use their intelligence and experience to fashion a beneficial way for the help-seeker to move forward in his life toward more meaningful activity.

Eighth, the value of *personal activity projects* is stressed in this scenario. The help-seeker had a number of activities to perform that would contribute to making his future a reality. Personal projects range from very small actions, such as making a telephone call, to large, complex projects, such as completing a program of study to qualify as a nurse. The important features of personal projects are that they are personally meaningful, feasible, and contributory to the help-seeker's goal and that they make sense from the point of view of the help-seeker.

Ninth, this series of three counselling sessions is a good example of *mindful problem solving*, demonstrating the following characteristics:

- The counsellor approached the help-seeker with an *experimental, playful* (humorous) *attitude*. This enabled both to be open to new ideas and cooperatively explore them. *New information was welcomed,* and it was integrated into personally useful knowledge on the part of both counsellor and help-seeker.
- *There was an implied recognition that there is more than one way to see things or solve problems.*
- Counselling enabled the help-seeker to *take more control over his existential context.*
- The *process of counselling*, including discussion, reflection time, information seeking, consultation, and feedback, was kept in the forefront and not subjugated to the demands of reaching a set goal.

- The *dialogic principle* of interpersonal communication was initiated and modelled by the counsellor and, to some extent, participated in by the help-seeker.

In this series of counselling conversations, an affirmative answer can be given to three questions: Did the participants engage in dialogical communication? Did the participants engage in problem solving? And, did the participants meta-communicate—keep track of their own contributions to the communication and use a range of communication tools? An affirmative answer to these questions means that this counselling process can be described as an *intelligent conversation*.

The conversation was not prescriptive, nor trivial, nor status-oriented. Instead, the counselling conversation included useful contributions from both participants in the service of investigating the life-space of the help-seeker and creating a possible future that the help-seeker could carry out and would find personally meaningful.

If there were a single key to success in this counselling process, it would be the respectful way that the counsellor *approached and validated the ongoing life experience of the help-seeker.* This enabled the two of them to find *common ground* in spite of a large gap in age and life experience.

From a SocioDynamic perspective, counselling is much more than a set of professional skills. It includes a world view, a philosophy of helping, and cultural tools for use in life planning and life-space reconstruction. Working as partners, helper and help-seeker help the latter seek answers to questions, such as, "What is going on in my existential life-space?" "How should I live my life?" "What are my options?" "What is my next step with regard to the concern I face?" "What new capacities do I need and how do I get them?" "Who can help me?" SocioDynamic counselling can be an inspired and inspiring way-of-being-in-the-world and implicates the counsellor in

- Constant self-education, development of a "helping self" that is able to implement co-constructive helping practices and remain open to new ideas about helping.

127

- Creation and continuous reconstruction of lifestyles that are self-creating, energizing, healthy, calm, and informed.
- Commitment to a holistic conception of helping that centres on life planning and reconstruction of self, relationships, and life-space and the validation of personal experience, choice, and capacity.
- A view of counselling as a transformative learning process within which individual self-creation and personal identity is fostered and valued.
- Showing a human face and respect for the constructive presence of the individual in his or her existential context as he or she is experiencing it.
- Valuing engagement in "intelligent" conversations as a way to produce better-than-ordinary solutions.

In conclusion, I believe that this counselling scenario points out two additional and important features of the SocioDynamic perspective. It demonstrates the *counsellor-as-bricoleur* at work. Mark and I had our own life experiences to contribute; the computer as a technical tool enabled us both to gather relevant, highly useful, and personally meaningful data, and we used this data to think together. Assembling this material-at-hand (experience, communication skill, data, life meanings), we pieced together a plan that Mark was able to follow and found a temporary solution to what he wanted to do in the immediate future.

Another important aspect of SocioDynamic counselling that this scenario illustrates is the importance of using, or building capacity to increase, the range of choices the help-seeker can make. This has the effect of extending the *personal freedom and fulfilment* of the help-seeker. In democratic and post-industrial societies, choice, opportunity, and goals that are valued by the individual should be within the reach of all citizens. By providing enhanced conditions of personal learning, the profession of counselling can help individuals to evaluate, revise, and re-author their perspectives on self, others, and society and then to decide and act on goals that are consistent with their desire for a respected and self-fulfilling life. I will conclude with a quote from an earlier book of mine.[57]

Counselling provides a person with the opportunity to examine the implications of her life as she is living it now and, thereby, to give consideration to alternative paths as she might live them in the future.

R. V. Peavy 1997

Endnotes

1. (1997). *SocioDynamic counselling: A constructivist perspective.* Victoria, Canada: Trafford Publishers; (1998). *Konstruktivistisk Vejledning: Teori og metode* (L. B. Jariskov, Trans.). Copenhagen, DK: Rådet for Uddannelses- og Erhevervsvejledning; (1999). *Sosiodynaaminen Ohjaus.* Helsinki: Psykologien Justannus Oy; (2000). *Træingshæfte i konstruktivistisk Vejledning: For Underfisere og Vejledere.* Copenhagen, DK: Rådet for Uddannelses-og Erhevervsvejledning.

2. I use the term *help-seeker* in preference to *client, customer,* or *patient.* Help-seeker directly describes the function of seeking help with a personal problem. Customer and client are terms widely used in business vocabularies and have the implication of economic value. Further, in earlier times, *client* implied dependency or leaning on another. In the middle ages, the term *client,* which is derived from the L. *clinare,* referred to vassals and serfs. *Patient* is part of the medical model vocabulary. Since I do not think that most people who come to counsellors should be regarded either as economic units or as sick, I believe that some term like help-seeker is a much more desirable designation for those who seek help.

3. The name *SocioDynamic Counselling* is a Canadian Trademark registered to Dr. R. Vance Peavy. Permission to use materials published under the name of SocioDynamic Counselling is freely granted to those wishing to use them as educational materials and to writers to quote reference materials published under the name *SocioDynamic.*

4. The term *psychopathologization* refers to the widespread tendency in the helping professions and, more generally, in media, to turn almost any human action or state of mind into a pathological condition. Thus we encounter such absurd phrases as the "average neurotic." In our post-Freudian world (*Psychopathology of Everyday Life*), pathology and abnormality are presumed to be everywhere. Metaphors of sickness and pathology have been criticized by Thomas Szasz, *The Myth of Mental Illness* (NY: Harper and Row, 1974); Susan Sontag, *Illness as a Metaphor* (NY: Farrar-Strauss, 1978); Ivan Illich, *Medical Nemesis* (NY: Random House, 1976).

5. The verb *objectify* means to cause to become or assume the characteristics of an object. From a SocioDynamic point of view, this is a categorical mistake. Humans are not objects, they are subjective or intersubjective in the sense of having the status as a being or becoming. Attempts to objectify a human being are not only a mistake, but both damaging and impossible.

131

6. A diagnostic label often places the diagnosed in an inferior and powerless position. In fact, one of the functions of counselling may be, in some instances, to de-diagnose. For example, I once saw a help-seeker who had been "diagnosed" as mentally retarded—a diagnostic label derived from an intelligence test—when he was in Grade 2. After that, he was referred to in the school records as an "MR," or as "delayed in development." These labels remained with him all the way through school and were the source of much pain and improper educational treatment. During our counselling, we found that he had a problem in reading that had never been discovered. He was of average intelligence and without developmental problems. When he finally learned to read, he was able to return to "normal" status without the damning labels. A great many diagnostic labels arise from testing. The SocioDynamic perspective is very conservative with regard to testing. Testing is an "industry" and driven by powerful economic interests. It also is used by institutions as a method of control. Testing offers a simple means of classification. However, it often works to the distinct disadvantage of the individual being tested. Occasionally there may be a legitimate reason for (psycho) diagnostic testing. For example, individual responses to a test of interests or a personality test, such as the Myers-Briggs Type Indicator, can be a source of valuable starting points for dialogue but not as a method of determining interest "profiles" or personality "types." Types and profiles should not become substitutes for individuality. Tests of personality, and tests more generally, incur the following five risks:

1. *Stigmatization.* Labels for deficiency, while notoriously vague, are dangerously permanent. The child diagnosed as having "attention deficit disorder" is not viewed as being in a position to judge the correctness of the label. He or she must accept the condition of being an "attention disordered child." Such a diagnosis places the individual on the margins of normalcy, perhaps never to be cured. It may mean to carry forever the stigma of self-enfeeblement, self-doubt, incompetence, and general deficiency.

2. *Reification.* Once diagnosed as schizophrenic, anorexic, mentally retarded, or neurotic, the individual is discussed, not in terms of his or her actual self and action, but in terms of the diagnostic label. Many children, diagnosed as slow learners in early grades, proceed throughout their school career as a diagnostic category (i.e., slow learners). The real self of the individual never becomes present to subsequent teachers.

3. *Individual blame.* Diagnosis places the malady inside the person, instead of inviting exploration of context, the workplace, family conditions, and so on. It is the individual who bears the label "not normal."

132

4. *Disempowerment of the person.* Diagnostic categories serve as power levers. The counsellor, teacher, psychologist, or physician can use the diagnosis to assert, "I know better than you because I have special power," conferred by the use of categories from which escape is nearly impossible. Diagnosis facilitates subjugation.

5. *Deterioration of relationship.* A diagnostic category serves as a signal for family, friends, and spiritual advisors to back off. The specialized language of diagnosis undermines cultural sensibility.

7. Peavy, R.V. (2002). Bibliographic essay on SocioDynamic Counselling. See: www.sociodynamic-constructivist-counselling.com

8. Bauman, Z. (2000). *Liquid modernity.* Cambridge: Polity Press. For further detailed discussions of how contemporary society is changing under the impact of globalization, conflict, migration, and technology, see Beck, U. (2000). *What is globalization?* (P. Camiller, Trans.). Cambridge: Polity Press; Giddens, A. (1991). *Modernity and self-identity.* Stanford: Stanford University Press; and Hage, J., & Powers, C. (1992). *Post-industrial lives.* Newbury Park: Sage.

9. Monk, G., Winslade, J., Crocket, K., & Epston, D. (Eds.). (1997). *Narrative therapy in practice: The archaeology of hope.* San Francisco: Jossey-Bass Publishers.

10. Anderson, H., Goolishian, H., Pulliam, G., & Winderman, L. (1986). The Galveston Family Institute: Some personal and historical perspectives. In D. Efron (Ed.), *Journeys: Expansions of the strategic-systemic therapies* (pp. 97-122). NY: Brunner/Mazel.

11. Schuster, S. (1999). *Philosophy practice: An alternative to counseling and psychotherapy.* Westport, CT: Praeger Publishers.

12. The intellectual era upon which we are entering in the beginning of this century is variously referred to as postmodern, late modern, post-postmodern, post-industrial, and so on. Each of these terms implies a leaving behind of the Modernist Myth of progress, the dominance of instrumental reasoning, and the end of rule by logical positivism. In the new millennium, it seems that we are entering into a new era, not only in terms of such phenomena as technology revolution and globalization but also in terms of world views and how we think about ourselves, others, and society. To some extent, I use the metaphor of "dialogical mind" as a counterpoint to the "industrial mind" that dominated the previous socio-historical period and still does to a lesser degree. In fact, most Western countries and cultures are a mix of

industrial thinking and postmodern and knowledge-society thinking. Castells (2000). *The rise of the network society* (2nd ed.), claims that we are entering into a truly interdependent, multicultural world, to which he gives the name, *Network Society*. He is concerned with the change of social structures on a global basis and how we must use pluralistic perspectives and multidisciplinary ideas if we are to comprehend what is happening in social life and respond intelligently to the challenges we face in this strange, new world. In my view, the SocioDynamic perspective is one example of a project that attempts to do just what Castells warns that we must do—revise our world views in the direction of plurality and respect for difference, using new vocabularies that do not put either people or machines in exclusive categories. We need to think our way into greater relatedness and ecological awareness and try to understand institutions as networks rather than as monolithic, enduring edifices.

13. The idea of "Guidance from the inside" is taken from the work of Timo Spanger (formerly Vähämöttönen) (1998). *Reframing career counselling in terms of counsellor-client negotiations.* Joensuu: University of Joensuu Publications in Social Sciences, N: O 34, p. 25.

14. Frankl, V. (1992). *Man's search for meaning.* Boston, MA: Beacon Press.

15. Rorty, R. (1989). *Contingency, irony, and solidarity.* NY: Cambridge University Press, p. 73.

16. Wittgenstein, L. (1976). *vermischte Bemerkungen.* (Translated as *Culture and Value*, G. H. Von Wright, Ed.). Oxford: Basil Blackwell. [Emphasis in this quote has been added].

17. Schaef, A. W. (1992). *Beyond therapy, beyond science.* San Francisco: Harper's, especially pp. 214-264.

18. The philosopher and historian of science, Thomas Kuhn, wrote about what he called "revolutionary science" and described how even in natural science there occur genuinely new causal stories and "paradigm shifts" in how a science is described and explained. New metaphors open up new ways of thinking about the world. In science and social science, as well as philosophy, it is by re-describing and using new metaphors that new knowledge and understandings are made.

19. Taylor, C. (1989). *Sources of the self.* Cambridge: Harvard University Press.

20. Rorty, R. (1989). *Contingency, irony, and solidarity.* NY: Cambridge University Press.

21. MacIntyre, A. (1984). *After virtue.* Notre Dame, IN: Notre Dame University Press.

22. For a convincing argument about the pretence of being scientific that is espoused by conventional schools of counselling and therapy, see Fancher, R. (1995). *Cultures of healing: Correcting the image of American mental health care.* NY: W.H. Freeman and Company.

23. Goffman, E. (1959). *The presentation of self in everyday life.* Garden City, NY: Doubleday. Also, see Goffman, E. (1967). *Interaction ritual: Essays on face-to-face behaviour.* Garden City, NY: Doubleday.

24. Martin Buber, a Jewish scholar and philosopher, is often called the "father of dialogue." His most important book is *I and thou* (1958). (2nd ed.) (W. A. Kauffman, Trans.). NY: Charles Scribner's Sons.

25. Sen, A. (1999). *Freedom as development.* NY: Alfred A. Knopf.

26. Unfreedoms constitute barriers to freedom. There are many *unfreedoms*, both contextual and internal. Lack of housing, food, health care, education, or opportunity for gainful employment, as well as denial of rights and exclusionary policies and doctrines, are examples of contextually or externally originating unfreedoms. Many persons effectively are put to the margins of society by such unfreedoms. Unfreedoms can also be internal and take the form of restrictive ideas, prejudices, incorrect assumptions, narrow perspectives, conflicted personal identity, unresolved emotional reactions, helplessness, blame, shame, and so on.

27. Maslow, A. (1968). *Toward a psychology of being.* NY: Van Nostrand.

28. Touraine, A. (1988). *Return of the actor: Social theory in postindustrial society.* Markham, ON: Fitzhenry & Whiteside.

29. Abram, D. (1996). *The spell of the sensuous.* NY: Pantheon Books.

30. Blackburn, S. (2000). *On being good.* Oxford: Oxford University Press.

31. Logstrup, K. (1997). *The ethical demand* (H. Fink & A. MacIntyre, Trans.). Notre Dame, IN: Notre Dame University Press, pp. 8-100, 148-158.

32. Bakhtin, M. (1984). *Problems of Dostoevsky's poetics.* Minneapolis, MN: University of Minnesota Press, pp. 59, 68, 110.

33. Jaspers, K. (1957). *Man in the modern age.* NY: Anchor Books.

34. Bateson, M. C. (1994). *Peripheral visions: Learning along the way.* NY: HarperCollins.

35. Vygotsky, L. (1994). In R. Van der Veer & J. Valsiner (Eds.), *The Vygotsky reader* (pp. 99-174). London: Basil Blackwell.

36. Steindl-Rast, D. (1983). *A listening heart.* NY: Crossroad, p. 10.

37. Rogers, C. (1969). *Freedom to learn.* Columbus, OH: Charles E. Merrill, p. 227.

38. An example of a practical guide for empathic listening is: Peavy, R. (1974). *Empathic listening workbook.* Victoria, BC: Adult Counselling Project.

39. Buber, M. (1947). *Between man and man.* London: Collins, p. 67.

40. Gusfield, J. R. (Ed.). (1989). *Kenneth Burke: On symbols and society.* Chicago: University of Chicago Press.

41. The way in which something shows itself (the other's meaning as we listen, for example) is discussed in a fundamental way by Martin Heidegger. See Heidegger, M. (1962). *Being and time* (J. Macquarrie & E. Robinson, Trans.). New York: Harper & Row, pp. 62-63.

42. Derrida, J. (1985). *The ear of the other.* NY: Schocken, p. 4.

43. I am indebted to the writings of Ellen Langer on mindfulness. I have adapted many of her ideas for use in helping practices. See Langer, E. (1989). *Mindfulness.* Reading, MA: Addison-Wesley.

44. Heidegger, M. (1962). *Being and time* (J. Macquarrie & E. Robinson, Trans.). New York: Harper & Row.

45. Touraine, A. (1988). *Return of the actor.* Minneapolis: University of Minnesota Press.

46. Vähämöttönen, T. (1998). *Reframing career counselling in terms of counsellor-client negotiations.* Joensuu, Finland: University of Joensuu Publications in Social Sciences.

47. Giddens, A. (1991). *Modernity and self-identity.* Stanford, CA: Stanford University Press.

48. Rogoff, B. (1995). Observing cultural activity on three planes: Participatory appropriation, guided participation, and apprenticeship. In J. Wertsch, P. Del Rio, & A. Alvarez, *Sociocultural studies of mind* (pp. 139-164). NY: Cambridge University Press.

49. Bakhtin, M. (1986). *Speech genres and other late essays* (V. McGee et al., Trans.). Austin, TX: University of Texas Press.

50. Clark, K., & Holquist, M. (1984). *Mikhail Bakhtin.* Cambridge, MA: Harvard University Press.

51. Bruner, J. (1987). Life as narrative. *Social Research, 54,* 11-32.

52. Lévi-Strauss, C. (1966). *The savage mind.* Chicago: University of Chicago Press.

53. Greenberg, L., & Watson, J. (1998). Experiential therapy of depression. Differential effects of client-centered relationship conditions and process-experiential interventions. *Psychotherapy Research, 8,* 210-224.

54. Bohart, A., & Tallman, K. (1999). *How clients make therapy work.* Washington, DC: American Psychological Association, pp. 239-241.

55. Rogoff, B. (1990). *Apprentice in thinking: Cognitive development in social context.* NY: Oxford University Press.

56. Castells, M. (2000). *The rise of the network society* (2nd ed.). Oxford: Blackwell Publishers.

57. Peavy, R. V. (1997). *SocioDynamic counselling: A constructivist perspective.* Victoria, Canada: Trafford Publishers, p. 17.

CPSIA information can be obtained
at www.ICGtesting.com
Printed in the USA
LVOW10s1838120218

566284LV00011B/17/P